SPIES OF THE OSS

SPIES OF THE OSS

ROBERT HAYDEN ALCORN

LONDON
ROBERT HALE & COMPANY

ISBN 0 7091 4001 0

Robert Hale & Company
63 Old Brompton Road
London S.W.7

Printed in Great Britain by
Clarke, Doble & Brendon Ltd.
Plymouth

CONTENTS

FOREWORD

FOR sheer courage, for daring, for physical and mental agility, and for the ultimate in selflessness there is no assignment to equal the work of the clandestine agent, whether spy or saboteur. It is also the most thankless of all occupations in terms of public recognition.

Glamourized in fiction, the spy or saboteur goes unmarked in real life until he is caught. It is an inverted world. The more successful a spy or saboteur becomes, the less he is known either for himself or his work. But should he fail, should he be caught, he is then despised and disowned.

Is there anyone who has not reacted with revulsion on reading the story of an uncovered espionage operation in the press? We resent the duplicity, the treachery, the betrayal of confidences. We overlook the courage, the loneliness, the living terror, the gnawing suspicion that some individual has made a part of his daily life in order to work for his country. For it is all there, whether the operative happens to be one of our own or from some other political entity. It is only within ourselves that the reaction differs.

The Office of Strategic Services was the World War II organization established by the U.S. Government for the recruiting, training, equipping, and operating of all clandestine activities of whatever kind against the enemy. It was in the spy and sabotage business, if you like.

Secrecy—security was the word used in the trade—is the core of such operations, and every man was trained to know only as much of his work, his organization, and the people

7

with whom he worked as would be necessary to the success of his own mission. Beyond that, all was limbo.

But a man long under tension must talk. There must be a release, and yet, within the bounds of security, he must be controlled. He can talk only with one who already knows the major facets of his operation.

I came in there. As the man responsible for the financing of clandestine operations of the OSS in the European Theatre, it was obviously necessary to know just a little more about the specifics of a mission in order to finance and supply it properly. It was only natural, therefore, that many returning agents, feeling the need to "talk it out," turned to me. They knew that I already knew the basics of their particular assignment. It would be no security violation, they reasoned, to fill in the details.

Every returning agent was pressed, probed for specifics. It was of vital importance to the OSS, its future operations, and its agents to know everything possible of enemy methods, to discover the strengths and weaknesses of each mission. Nothing could be overlooked, nothing could be left out.

These stories come from that source.

The reader is asked only to remember that all of these "tales" are true. These people were actual operatives of the OSS, trained by us, despatched to the field by us, and fully committed to the most dangerous of all conceivable assignments. I knew every one personally, and some were close friends.

And if the tensions at times seem unbearable, if the horrors and the dangers and the strange twists stretch the credulity, one can only say that there are many more stories infinitely more harrowing and less believable, but true for all that. They shall remain untold.

At this date, years after the war, it may seem strange that fictitious names are used. The only way to reply to that is to emphasize that this was a game played for keeps and one can never tell when some long harboured grudge against an agent may explode in violence to his family or friends. This we hope to avoid.

It would seem that these young men and women gave quite enough, without carrying any threat to others.

CHAPTER ONE

DE BRIELLE

H E sat alone at a little table in a corner of the dark, damp
bistro, the humid fog of ersatz cigarette smoke, sodden uniforms, and unclean bodies pressing round him in a wine-sour
grey haze. There was a half-filled glass of red wine in front of
him, and he idly, almost vacantly, traced a finger through a
wet blot on the marble top of the table.

Well over six feet when drawn to full height, his figure
in the layers of cheap, heavy clothing, spoke of strength
and muscle and coordination in direct contradiction to the
blankness of the face. The strong nose, wide brow, firm
jaw, and that strange combination of clear, bright-pink
cheeks and the dull, blue-black cast of a potentially heavy
beard made the face now young, now old, impossible to date.
Only the dark, vacant, expressionless eyes seemed out of tune,
as though they belonged to another face. The age? Who could
tell? The mid-to-late twenties perhaps, or even the early
thirties. The bland, unseeing face, uncomprehending, uncom-
mitted, told nothing.

The room was crowded with men in the heavy field uniform
of the German officer. There was a sign just outside the door,
in German, indicating that this bistro was reserved for officers
only. It had a better grade of wine, better cheese, a small stove
for heat, and an agreeable proprietress. At least she had proven
less sullen than most. After all, France had been occupied by
the Germans for some three years, and the strain was showing
in every facet of life. It made the interludes like this seem
somehow an oasis of content, or at least a setting for moments
of carefree banter.

There were several clusters of officers smoking and drinking,
laughing and joking. Occasionally one of them would glance
perfunctorily toward the solitary figure at the table in the

9

corner as if looking at a piece of furniture. One, a major, called loudly to the *patronne* in his German-accented French, and she came around from behind the bar and over to his table.

The major gave his order and the *patronne* poured a fresh glass of the heavy wine at the bar. When she came back to the major he was writing on a small slip of paper from his wallet and ignored her presence until he had finished. Then, as if surprised that she was there, he looked up, slipped the pencil into his inside pocket, and placed the leaf of paper on the small tin tray that she held toward him with the glass of wine.

She went directly to the lonely figure at the table in the corner. He seemed not to notice her approach, and she stood squarely in front of him, blocking his view of the rest of the room, before he looked up. She smiled, placed the small glass of wine on the table in front of him, and then with a deliberate emphasis put the note beside the glass. He glanced at the glass, at the note, and smiled back at her. He took the note between his fingers and tilted it so that he could read what it said. The script was large and somehow it looked improbable, slightly ridiculous, the French words in the strangely patterned German writing.

"*A votre santé.*"

He looked up at her again, still smiling, and she gestured broadly toward the German major and his companions at the table across the room. They had all turned their attention to him now and were waiting expectantly for his acknowledgment.

He lifted his glass, held it up and smiled. As one man the major and his officers lifted their glasses in a similar gesture. Then, together, they drank each other's health.

The *patronne* skittered back to the bar. There was a rustled resettling among the officers' group, and he was left to himself again. The empty, unseeing look returned to his face, and he sat almost motionless over his drink. Then, slowly, automatically, he lifted the glass, sipped the wine, and settled back into his silent world.

Twenty minutes passed and he rose slowly from his chair, found the money for his first drink, and placed it on the table by the empty glasses. He turned up the collar of his coat, thrust his hands into his pockets, and shuffled slowly towards the door. No one seemed to notice. The German major and his friends, absorbed in their own pleasures, turned not a glance toward him as he sidled past the crowded tables.

He pushed open the door with the pressure of his shoulder and stepped into the darkening street. He stood for a moment on the sidewalk, his face lifted up to the fresh cleanliness of the rain before walking down the street and letting the night absorb him.

It had been a long road.

And only he, Alain de Brielle, would ever know, could ever know in detail just how long, how arduous, how dangerous the road leading to that small bistro had been. Nor could anyone other than himself fully assess the value of that proffered glass with its trite note "A votre santé." It meant more to him than any decoration could ever mean, simply because it was proof of the success of his mission.

I had first known Alain in the prewar years when I had been a student at Cambridge University in England and later at the Ecole des Sciences Politiques in Paris. One of a large and prominent French family, Alain had been given advantages not often offered to the young student in prewar France. His early schooling had been, of course, in France. But then there had been three years of formal education in England, there had been a year in Germany, a year in Italy, and two short vacation trips to America. The result of all of this exposure had been the creation of a young man worldly, self-reliant, informed, and adaptable beyond the usual, to say the least. With the exception of perhaps one other Frenchman of my acquaintance, Alain de Brielle spoke better English than any foreigner I ever knew. His accent was so clipped and British in its inflection, he was able to pass in England without the slightest query as to his nationality. His Italian was outstanding, and his ability with German was almost as good. Coupled with his amazing language facility, Alain had a keen, highly alert and perceptive mind, great intelligence, and a sharp and disarming sense of humour. On the physical side he stood a little over six feet tall and controlled a body that had been well conditioned by tennis and riding to the point of semiprofessional excellence.

This, then, was the boy who was impressed into the French army when the German panzers first roared to the west in the early days of the war. Like that of many another young Frenchman, his actual service as a soldier of France was brief, bitter, and sad. And though France as a military force was early out of the conflict, young Alain de Brielle within himself decided to fight on in whatever way was left open to him.

I never did find out how he got to England. Whenever the subject came up, he would only smile and say, "I knew the right people. It was not so very difficult." And yet there was something about the tone and the look behind the eyes that led one to believe that there was a saga hidden there more complicated, of more daring and perseverance, hardship and cunning than one could ever guess.

Our own meeting, in London, was as casual as if we had only seen each other a few days previously. I was walking down Grosvenor Street toward OSS headquarters one afternoon when he came towards me from the opposite direction. He was wearing the uniform of a lieutenant in the Free French Army, and I was then a major in the U.S. forces. There was that sudden, quick moment of disbelief on the part of each of us, and then in a torrent of excitement and enthusiasm, the lapse of the past five years had vanished and we were together again.

Even with one's closest friends one was always cautious in the OSS. So, instead of taking him on to the office with me, I turned him into Davis Street, circled the block, and took him into the Connaught Hotel for a drink. I can remember feeling a twinge of disloyalty to our friendship by my action. After all, here was a young man whom I had known for years, we had been students together, we had gone on trips and vacations together, we had been almost as close as brothers, and yet I was instinctively protecting my position, covering my tracks until I could be absolutely sure, after a lapse of years, that we were in the same playing field. For an intelligence operative, never is one's sense of isolation so great as when dealing with an old friend in whom one dare not confide.

He was healthy and fit, and he was chafing at the endless days of inactivity he was finding in London with the Free French. "Waiting. We're always waiting. For what I don't know nor really care," I remember his saying. "All I know is that it is driving me crazy, this waiting." And so we parted, having arranged to meet for lunch three days hence.

Still cautious, I had asked Alain to meet me at the U.S. Officers' Mess so that he would not have any idea as to where I was working. I had told him at the first meeting that I was doing a humdrum desk job in an Army headquarters spot and let it go at that. But in the meantime I had taken the precaution to have a security check made on him through our own offices and was able to verify everything he had told me. I felt considerably easier therefore at this lunch meeting.

He was as enthusiastic, as bursting with energy as he had been during his student days, and he was full of all kinds of ideas as to what he could do for the war effort if only given the chance. The gist of it was that he would be willing to do anything, but most of all he would like to go to parachute school and then be dropped behind enemy lines into occupied France.

"After all," that modulated voice said in the impeccable British accent, "what good is a bloody Frenchman in England? A Frenchman's value now is in France."

That did it.

I went from that lunch straight back to my office and started a full security clearance investigation on one Alain de Brielle. General Donovan, the head of the Office of Strategic Services, happened to be in London at the time, and I discussed the possibility of using de Brielle with him. As I knew he would, he approved the idea provided the clearance was all right, pointing out that one of the strongest bonds one could have in an intelligence network was a background of close personal friendship.

A few days later the clearance came through. It bore out everything I knew of Alain, and it showed even more. It showed a good background of military training prior to his active service: It showed a good record of active service, and although it too drew a blank as to how he had got into England, it showed that he was held in high regard by his fellow officers in the Free French forces in London.

There is a tremendous interplay of emotions when one is recruiting a close friend for a hazardous espionage assignment. I experienced them all. I knew that Alain would make a magnificent agent. I knew that I could use him for that most crucial of all information, data on the safety of the currencies it was my job to provide for all of our espionage and sabotage operations. And I knew that any assignment that could produce such information would be delicate, dangerous, and desperately tedious. I knew that I could keep quiet, and that he would in all probability eventually find himself an equally hazardous assignment. I also knew that I would not keep quiet—rather that I would approach him with a definite plan, an offer to work for me in the OSS.

It was perhaps two weeks after our first chance meeting on Grosvenor Street that Alain had dinner with me. In the turmoil and hubbub of the officers' mess there was no chance to talk seriously, and our conversation was mostly about past experiences and what we had each been doing up to the outbreak of war. It was one of those soft evenings in early spring that only England can produce, and we crossed Park Lane after dinner and strolled slowly through Hyde Park. I was anxious that Alain propose himself for an assignment, for we had early learned that only the dedicated volunteer makes a first-class agent on an espionage mission. It was not difficult. Again he was chafing, and again he was saying that he would really like to go back to France, not just as a soldier but in a special capacity, in some way that would take advantage of what he himself felt he had to offer.

I plunged.

I steered him to a nearby bench. It sat openly beside one of the many wide paths across the park so that I could see clearly in all directions. In rough outline I told him, not of my own job, but that I knew of a spot where he might be helpful, that he could be helping me as well as the whole war effort. I emphasized the dangers involved : that there would be a long period of strenuous, tedious training; that there would be infinite details to master; that the work, once begun, could be brutal in its isolation; that he was in plain language offering his very life.

There would have been no need for him to speak. The excited lustre of his eyes, the tensed forward leaning of his body as I spoke, the eager flexing of his fingers, they all told more than words that here was a young man keyed to the bursting point to meet challenge and danger.

The vastness of the park, a miracle of open country in the middle of London, with its fields of lawn and enormous trees, its shrubs and flowers, was slowly disintegrating into the shadows. The barbed-wire and slat fencing, the Nissen huts, the ugly earthworks of the anti-aircraft gun emplacements, they were all fading with the light into indistinct lumps of shapeless greens, then grey-blues, violet, and then deep blue-black.

We agreed to meet at my flat the next morning to arrange details and rose to leave. It was almost black night as we left the park and reached the wide challenge of Park Lane. One could hear the traffic, but only as one got to the very edge of the road could the tiny points of light that passed for headlights be seen. We made it safely across, and at the corner of Upper Grosvenor Street we shook hands and parted.

Alain was whistling as he vanished into the dark. I stood for a moment and listened, and then, when I could no longer hear him, I turned and went down Grosvenor Street in the blackout. I always rather enjoyed the black, the lost feeling, the mystery of passing forms that one only heard and never saw, the navigation by ear rather than by sight, the approaching click of heels on pavement, the brush past, and the receding sound. I crossed a side street, and in the next block a lone cigarette glowed in the doorway of a house, there was the slight jingle of keys, then silence. Farther along there was another glow of cigarette, brighter and more prolonged, and I smiled to myself at the ingenuity of the adaptable London streetwalker.

As I crossed Grosvenor Square, now ugly with the wire fencing, the huts, and the fat silver laziness of the barrage balloons, mercifully obscured by the night, I heard the first distant wail of an alert siren, and then, like a chain reaction, I could hear them coming closer and closer until the sirens around the square were going and all of London was in a wail. The figures one passed were moving faster now, not running, just moving faster, and above the tomcat wail of the sirens one could hear the distant, menacing drone of the bombers coming in and the distant *woof* and *whump* of the anti-aircraft guns.

I walked more quickly, only partially aware that it was easier now because there was a dull glow against the sky. Then, with no warning whatsoever, there was a kind of sucking in and blowing out like an enormous bellows at work, followed instantly by the deafening boom and chatter of the Bofors guns just up the street in the park. Searchlights had now come up, crossing and recrossing the sky, feeling and probing in the murk. I stopped for a moment and watched. Suddenly they had one, a plane pinned against the sky in the cross beams of light no bigger and no more menacing than a moth and, while the lights held him a moving prisoner, everything was thrown at it. Then a merciful cloud obscured the plane and it was lost to view, while below all of London wailed and roared, flamed and boomed its defiance.

I went quickly into my flat.

De Brielle began his training.

It was arranged that he would be sent to one of our own OSS schools where the physical toughening that was basic to any espionage or sabotage operation could be developed. There was a bit of delicate negotiation to release him from the Free French forces and impress him into our own service. But fortunately General Donovan and Col. David Bruce, head of the OSS in the ETO, had worked out a pattern for such exchange with the highest officials of the French government-in-exile. It was all done on a gentleman's-agreement basis that left the minimum of traceable evidence. The mission had begun.

He was conditioned with long hikes in rugged country. He was taught how to fight. Not the aim-and-shoot kind of fighting taught the regular military trainee—that was basic, already part of the equipment. Now he was taught the tough, gouging, death-dealing treachery of judo, garroting, and the like. He had jump training, endless trips in harness to the dizzying height of a jump scaffold, learning how to jump, how to free-fall and how to land—all this from a pylon before he was ready to do it for the first time from a plane. Then the endless jumps, over and over again through the "joe-hole" of the converted bomber. There were survival assignments when he was abandoned in the wilds of the Scottish Highlands for days, fending for himself, living off the land, finding food and shelter as best he could, and always running the risk, even then, of being shot by some well-meaning Scot on the assumption that he was a landed enemy airman or spy.

He was as lean, taut, and muscular as a racing greyhound when I next saw him. His basic conditioning was over, and he was now ready for special training. And already the super-strict security that was to ensure the safety of his mission was beginning to close in. This calls for some explanation. The OSS maintained a series of areas for the conditioning and training of its espionage and sabotage agents. The larger of these areas were concerned mainly with the physical honing of the trainees; they were handled in large groups, and they might or might not be enrolled under their actual names. There was a great deal of sifting and winnowing at these areas, and only the really durable ones made it to the next grade. From the very beginning every trainee was observed and assessed in every way until there was nothing that was not known about him. Any weakness, and quirk, or fault was noted and rated as to its effect on the over-all make-up of the ideal agent. More than muscle, stamina, and physical coordination would be needed. Nerve, cool calculation under stress, mental alertness, the fine art of dissimulation, these too were of vast importance. And when all these factors had been assessed and tallied, a candidate was either "washed out" or sent on to more specialized training.

Alain was a high man on the candidate roster. I had expected it and was already making plans for the specifics of his mission. There was a short vacation of a few days in London after he completed his basic training and before he began the intensive, gruelling study for his special mission. It was then that he came to me with his own idea for his "cover", an idea that left me aghast at its complexity. He would, he explained disarmingly, go into France as a deaf-mute.

I rebelled at the idea. In the first place, one of the basics on which the successful espionage agent operates is the idea of being inconspicuous. Anything that separates one from the crowd, anything that makes one stand out or draws attention immediately, of itself, creates a danger. To be marked is to be observed, to be observed is to be followed, to be followed is to be suspect, and to be suspect is to be, if not dead, at least rendered valuless to the network.

On the other hand the very specialness of Alain's idea was intriguing. His arguments were convincing. As a deaf-mute, he insisted, he would be regarded as harmless. Interrogation, which would have to be done with pad and pencil, would become too tedious to be pursued. He would pose as one so slow-witted as to be unable to utilize any type of sign language, and even his spelling and grammar would be unskilled. It would explain away his being free of war involvement, and it would leave him the opportunity to obtain employment where his physical ability would mean more than his apparent lack of mental agility. And since he was to operate as a "loner," without any team mate, he could be trained and schooled for his assignment privately.

We took the risk.

Alain was given intensive training in codes and ciphers, in the sending and receiving of radio messages and, essentially, the repair, rebuilding, and construction of communications sets. He learned how to pick locks, how to blow safes. He was taught how to rifle files and go through a desk leaving no trace of his presence, even to the replacement of dust on a smooth surface. This was the easy part.

What was infinitely more difficult was the tremendous self-discipline required for his submersion into the role of a deaf-mute. He steeled himself to accept the most startling noises, the most sudden surprises as if they were in a world remote from his own. At first he tried earplugs and then, as he gained confidence, he removed them as he knew he would have to and could sit stolidly through an ordinary day, writing his every communication with others, making no sound, pretending to hear no sound, until even I had begun to think that he might have actually become a deaf-mute. Air-raid sirens, anti-aircraft guns, falling bombs, these and a thousand other noises he accepted without a quiver of recognition.

Then, one day, when I found myself automatically reaching for pad and pencil to begin our "talk," I realized that the deception was complete, that the mission was ready to begin in earnest.

Everything was now moving faster, focussed in on Alain and his operation. The clothing, from underwear out, had been made for him in our own OSS workrooms, and it had even been suitably and subtly scuffed, stained, faded, and patched into the likeness of thousands of other outfits one might find in occupied France. Our documents section furnished him the necessary ration cards, identity cards, work cards and the like, again suitably ruffled and mutilated to avoid suspicion. And there were even small packets of French notepaper, cheap and greyed, with small, cheap French pencils for his deaf-mute correspondence with anyone he might meet.

The night he left on his mission, I went out to the airfield with him. We were a small group and we had an excellent dinner together before Alain was dressed up for his drop. This was a crucial part of the dispatch of an agent because it was the final chance to check all clothing, all equipment, everything, for any tell-tale flaw that might break the cover and endanger the mission. Through it all Alain spoke not a word, gave not a sign that he heard a sound. Perhaps three of us knew his secret, but the others, the jump crew who would ride with him and had been instructed to tap him on the shoulder as his signal to jump when over target, the pilot, the ground crew, they all accepted and admired him as a deaf-mute.

How much they admired him was expressed in one word uttered by a sergeant standing nearby as he entered the plane. In his jump smock, camouflaged, with his chute, his knife, and his gun, Alain turned to me at the steps of the plane and held out his hand. His eyes were wide-flaring with excitement, and he grasped my hand and held it for what seemed a long minute. Then, quickly, he clambered aboard the plane, turned at the door, and with a quick smile made the famous Churchill V-sign. There was a courage, a defiance and assurance in the smile and the gesture that seemed to surge over our small group and filled us with a sudden pride. The sergeant gave it a vocal recognition. "Christ."

The jump crew reported that the drop had been easy. The pilot had brought them in on target, they had clearly seen the tiny pinpoints of light sent up by the reception party on the ground to guide Alain to his landing, and they were well away without any incident. Three days later we received the terse signal from Alain that he had landed safely, that everything was routine. He was operational.

Because of his superior intelligence, his nerve, and his knowledge of the country, we had given Alain almost complete freedom in the setting up of his mission. My own confidence in him was such that I knew we had only to wait. I was sure he would produce.

The Germans were playing diabolical games with the currencies then circulating in France. Suddenly, and without warning, they would declare a whole series of five-thousand-franc notes invalid on the assumption that any enemy agent who might have been supplied with such notes from outside France would be in grave danger of detection or would be operationally destitute. Our own agents were, for the most part, supplied with francs purchased in the black market in Lisbon. These would be notes often flown into Lisbon by the Germans themselves to be used in foreign exchange and, since they were fresh from the Bank of France, it was easy for the German authorities to keep listings of series, denominations, and the like. On a moment's notice they could set a trap for an unwary agent. The Gestapo was constantly pulling "money raids", quick searches of a shop, a small business, or a private house or individual for the dual purpose of discovering illicit funds and terrorizing the people.

All of this and more we had explained to Alain. It was up to him, by any means he could devise, to discover whatever he could of the German manipulation of currency in occupied France. It meant, quite obviously, that his main operational base would be Paris.

In any mission there is an agonizing period of waiting, long days and weeks of anxious uncertainty, after that first communication stating only that the agent has arrived and is at work.

It takes time. Time. Patience. Slow, step-by-step, cautious intrusion into some spot, some locale, some toehold from which to begin the dangerous game of gathering intelligence. All this I knew. I also knew that many a good agent simply vanishes, sometimes. Vanishes without a trace, simply a silence in that tenuous radio contact. Then the silence becomes heavy and loud, then dull, and then an accepted thing, a strangely intangible death.

His first message was typical. It read, tersely, "Rumour Gestapo recalling all five thousand franc notes. Rumour only. Will check." It was signed with his code "O".

As far as I was concerned, that single letter "O" was of more importance than the message that preceded it. We had agreed on his code because, as he had said, "It is O for Zero. I have come full circle." And out of that statement had come our device by which he might signal us if he were captured and sending messages under duress. As a freely operating agent his signals would be signed with the single "O". But there had to be precautions against the chilling possibility that he might be captured and that the Germans might just wish, for their own uses, to keep him in contact with us while they tried to break our code or discover other links to our chain. In such a condition it was agreed that Alain would sign "O for Zero".

It was in September 1943 that Alain de Brielle had first been dropped into occupied France. And from that first terse message in late October, the information that he produced for us became increasingly more voluminous, accurate, and delicate. We decided to bring him out for a few days of briefing in London in March 1944.

Only then did I get the full story of his mission.

The complexity, the immense detail involved in the accomplishment of any espionage assignment, is almost beyond comprehension. But certain basics must be understood by the lay reader if he is to make any sense out of the "how" of such a mission. Through early operational contacts, through the resistance workers and the underground movement within occupied France, scattered pools of friendly and sympathetic men and women stood ready to aid in the reception and early protection of a dropped agent. This is perhaps his most vulnerable moment. After all a single plane, flying low over isolated countryside is, even in the dark of night, not an ideal beginning for a clandestine mission. It is imperative, therefore, that there be ground agents, loyal personnel in the area who will be able to assist an arriving agent. They outline the drop area by a prearranged system of pinpoint lights; they gather and bury immediately any equipment arriving with the agent; they contact him and take him to a safe house at some distance from the drop site; in fact they do everything possible to minimize the dangers.

Alain was well received on the ground. And for the first time since his intensive training had begun, he broke his role as a deaf-mute. It was all part of the plan to ensure the success of his mission. After all, it had been reasoned, there was a clean break from plane to ground, so that there could be no traceable query as to this sudden change. Secondly, in those early hours, in the dark, speech would be vital to safety. Thirdly, Alain was planning to work far from his drop site. At the most he would spend forty-eight hours in the countryside near the drop area and, once out of there and lost in the depths of Paris, it would be easy to change once again into the deaf-mute he had trained himself to be.

It worked.

He was met, on landing, and taken with few words to a small farmhouse near the drop area. Two men went with him and, in the warmth and dim light of the kitchen, they proved to be a father-son combination. There was a plump, pleasant farmwife in the kitchen, and she gave him a large bowl of soup from the stove, huge chunks of bread from her own ovens, some home-made cheese, and red wine. All three were obvious sophisticates at this game of harbouring newly dropped agents. They struck just the right note of confidence. They were friendly, but they asked no unnecessary questions. There was no mention of where he had come from, there was no talk of war. There was only the assurance that he could safely stay with them for as long as he wished, that he would be warmly bedded and he would be fed.

Alain stayed that night. And as he at last cushioned himself into a large bed, he admitted to himself that he was as relaxed as if he had come home. He slept late, and he stayed hidden all of the next day. It bothered him slightly that he felt so at ease, that there was no tension, no awareness of danger, and he slept the second night with the soundness of a child. The following morning he left some chocolate and cigarettes with the family and rode into the nearest town on a dumpcart-load of manure. It was driven by his host and pulled by one of those tremendous French draught horses. He didn't see the family again until he was picked up for his return to London in the following March.

He bought a used bicycle in the town. He couldn't have got a new one had he been foolish enough to want one. There were no new bicycles available, and the one he got was only barely serviceable. The frame was rusted and bent, the tyres were dry and cracked and had been patched. All the better, so long as it could be ridden.

He was miles from Paris, but that was his secondary objective. There was a small village, once rural, but with the inevitable encroachment of the spreading city and its suburbs, busier and less isolated than when he had known it as a boy. It was familiar territory, it was friendly territory. It was more than that. Away from the main street of the little town with its rows of stone houses, at the end of a small, rutted and tangled lane, there was a small farm. The stone house was attached and looked like a mere appendage to the larger stone barn. There was a walled yard, a small poultry house, and a shed for swine. And there were two people, the Veyzacs, who were almost like family to him.

Marie Veyzac had been a nurserymaid in the de Brielle family for years. She had nursed and tended Alain almost from birth, and she had stayed with the family until she had married. Gustave Veyzac, the man she married, had been a farmhand on the de Brielle estate; he had been born there, and he had stayed with them until his marriage. With what they had both saved, the Veyzacs had bought the small farm hoping to raise a brood of their own. However, children were denied the former nursemaid for some reason, and Marie and Gustave lived quietly and contentedly with their cows, their pigs, their chickens, ducks, and geese, their workhorses.

But the contact had never been broken. Like homing pigeons, the Veyzacs made semi-annual pilgrimages to the de Brielle estate in Touraine. And whenever any of the de Brielle family needed help with a nursery problem, Marie was eager and willing to go to them. Alain knew he could count on their assistance as surely as if they were blood relations.

Their small farm, then, was his destination. He made the trip in a day without serious incident. Only once, as he cycled through a larger town, was he stopped. A Nazi patrol, apparently on a routine checkup, halted him and asked him for his papers. Even as the Nazi spoke, Alain brought forth his pad and pencil, handed them to the astonished German, and made gestures to indicate that he was deaf and dumb. The German scribbled "Carte d'Identité" on the paper, held it toward him, and waited for him to fumble for his papers. He only scanned them, handed them back, along with his pad and pencil, and motioned him on his way. Alain casually arranged his papers, tucked them in his pocket, mounted his bicycle, and rode slowly away without looking back. He could feel his heart pulsing erratically, and his face felt flushed, but he kept going with the dull indifference of a semi-idiot.

The narrow lane leading to the farm was too rough and rutted for a bicycle, and he had to dismount and wheel his cycle beside him. He had long since planned his whole approach to Marie and Gustave. At first he had thought he would carry the deaf-mute act to them, explaining his condition by an incident in his war service. There were two dangers in this. First Marie and Gustave knew the family too well, it would be too easy for them to discover the deception, for they would have known of any injury to him serious enough to rob him of speech and hearing. Further, he realized that to deceive them in this manner would weaken his position with regard to their confidence. He must trust them either completely or not at all. The fact that they lived alone, without children, an isolated, quiet existence, was an advantage. His real operation was to be in Paris, in an area where he would know no one. The Veyzac farm would be only a haven, a place to go on occasion to break the tension and, if all went well, a place from which he could contact London.

Gustave was in the barnyard when Alain arrived. He was

leading a huge, feather-footed horse, just unhitched from a large farm cart, into the stable. He was only aware of Alain's presence and, without recognizing him or knowing to whom he was speaking he called out a curt greeting as he disappeared into the stable ahead of the bulk of the horse. Alain leaned his bicycle against a wall and followed man and horse into the warm, strong-scented gloom of the building. Gustave studied him for a moment as if unsure. The beret, the faded, patched work clothes, the heavy *sabots*, these were not clothing he associated with Alain de Brielle. It was only when Alain spoke that he knew.

The welcome was warm and sincere. And when Gustave had finally recovered from the shock and excitement of seeing Alain, he took him on into the house, where Marie was just beginning to prepare the evening meal. She was overcome and burst into tears at the sudden appearance of her "baby". She kept hugging him, then standing away, brushing her eyes and smiling and then, rushing forward, enveloping him in her fat arms, holding him against her huge bosom and rocking him back and forth.

How? Where? Why? The questions tumbled out of her with no sequence, no logic. Sit here. No, there. Nearer the fire. Take off your *sabots*. Wine, yes, wine. Or something hot, yes, something hot. Cold hands, your hands are cold. I'll get a pillow, you must be tired. Alain was prodded, bossed, petted, and queried all at once in a flurry of motherly tenderness.

He stayed only two nights and a day with the Veyzacs. It was time enough. He learned his way about the farm. He noted its position in relation to the other farms nearby, in relation to the road. He studied the building, the stone barn, the smaller poultry house, the haystacks, even the huge pile of manure that attested to the wealth of the farm. And he told Marie and Gustave only what they needed to know. He told them that he was going to Paris, that he had business there, that he would be gone some time, that he would certainly be back if it was all right with them. There was no mention of his real assignment, nor was there any indication that he had ever left France. As far as Marie and Gustave Veyzac knew, he had been in France ever since the collapse, perhaps as a prisoner, perhaps in a work gang; these were things that happened, but of which no one spoke unless the information was volunteered. He asked only one favour: that they mention his arrival to no one, not even to any member of his family, or any past or present employee of the estate. They promised to keep his secret.

Paris was a different matter.

It was seething with Germans. Nazis, SS men, the Gestapo, officers and men, they were everywhere. And so was the swastika. Black, white, and red, the hated emblem floated over Paris like a vile excrescence, it hung flat and menacing against the façades of buildings, it was stamped on public notices, it was on armbands, it was everywhere.

The gaiety of prewar Paris was gone, and in its place was a sullen, drab, and humiliated populace. The mad cacophony of taxi horns had given way to the metallic clatter of German army vehicles. ACHTUNG! HALT! SIEG HEIL! HEIL HITLER! These were the punctuation marks to daily life, the accompaniment to all that grey, the grey of uniform, the grey of sky, the grey of despair, the grey of regimentation, the black-grey of terror.

It was this, more than any other single thing about Paris, that struck Alain. No one trusted anybody. The French hated the Germans, the Germans hated the French, and neither trusted the other. What was infinitely worse, Frenchmen distrusted Frenchmen, and even the German conquerors distrusted each other. Resistance workers, Maquis, *collaborateurs*, every Frenchman, every Frenchwoman, every French child was actually or potentially one or the other. SS Gestapo, Elite Guard or *Abwehr*, every German had his private allegiance to one or the other. It was a living, haunting hell of distrust.

Alain lost himself in the very centre of the seething pool of hate. And for the first twenty-four hours he simply wandered, sensing the place, listening without seeming to hear, absorbing the poison of the atmosphere and building within himself a hate he never knew was there. He needed a room, and yet he dared not yet make the moves necessary to find a place to live. So he wandered. The Métro stations and the parks and gardens were closed at night, so he was forced to sleep in odd crannies, bridge abutments on the quays by the Seine, shop doorways on the smaller streets, the darkest recesses of a church, but never twice in the same place. Those were the nights.

The days were spent in a purposeful hunt for the place to strike. With typical German efficiency and bravado, every headquarters building was clearly labelled and blatantly draped with swastikas. It was not difficult to discover where the Gestapo held forth. It was in an area where he knew it would be impossible to find a cheap furnished room, so he began his search farther afield. It would be better cover not to live too near his operating base, and yet, what he had seen of Paris made him realize that the more exposure he gave himself in the streets, the greater the danger.

His plan, daring and bold in the extreme, was quite simply to present himself at Gestapo headquarters and apply for a job as a janitor. What he hoped for was the night shift, but he was astute enough to know that to ask for night work would immediately arouse suspicion. Furthermore, it would be impossible to get work until he had a place to live. Almost the first question to be asked would be his address, and it was only safe to suppose, in occupied Paris, such an address would be checked and confirmed.

He found something on the Left Bank. The street was narrow, dark, and dirty, the building itself was dingy, and there was a peeling, cracked sign "Hôtel" over a frosted-glass door with a smaller sign saying "By week or month". It would be difficult to say whether it was a bona-fide cheap hotel or an even cheaper brothel. He went past it several times before he went inside. It was near a corner on a short street. Best of all it was in an area of Paris he knew well from his student days, all of which would be important should the worst happen and he had to run for it some night.

He went inside. There was a strong stink of foul air in the hall, a mixture of stale cooking, sewage, and stale sweat, and he almost turned and left. Only the realization that this was the sort of environment he required kept him going. There was a dim light to the left showing through more frosted glass, there was a counter-like desk, and there was a woman seated behind it. She was knitting. Her hair was grey, thin, and stringy, and her face was wrinkled and heavily made up, the lipstick showing skip marks in the cracks around her mouth. There were a few teeth in the mouth, only a few.

Alain took out his pad and wrote that he required a room, by the month if possible. He slid the paper toward her and watched her reaction.

The woman looked at him quizzically and kept on talking even though he had written on the paper that he was *un mute*. She was quoting rates, telling him how scarce good rooms were to come by, what a fine clientele she had, and numerous other items that he pretended not to hear. She laboriously wrote some of it on his pad and passed it back to him. He read it slowly and then pointed to the words "small room, first floor, rear, 450 francs".

The woman took some keys from a rack by the desk, came around into the hall, and motioned him to follow. They went down a narrow, dark, stinking hall. There was ragged brown linoleum on the floor, and there was a kind of brown linoleum wainscoting along the lower walls. It gave a glazed, dank feeling to the hall and made the clack of their heels sound almost metallic. She unlocked a door at the end of the hall and went inside. There was one window, and though it was mid-afternoon there was hardly enough light in the room to see the contents. She pulled the chain of the only overhead light in the room, a single bare bulb, and illuminated a sagging double bed, a chair, a washstand, and wardrobe with a cracked door.

He pulled back the bed clothing and sniffed at the sheets in search of the tell-tale odour of bedbugs.

"Pas de puces, Monsieur. Pas de puces."

She screamed at him. But when he remained inert, uncomprehending, she snatched at the pad in his hand, took a pencil from her hair, and wrote the words, underlined.

Alain punched the thin mattress. Then, under the words the woman had written about the fleas, he wrote 400. She read as he formed the figures and she was screaming *Non, Non,* even before he had finished. She kept screaming it at him, enraged at his calm, unhearing manner, shaking her head, gesticulating and finally, in desperation, writing "NON, NON, NON".

He shrugged his shoulders and started out of the room. He walked slowly, lethargically down the hall, and then he could hear her coming quickly behind him. He plodded on to the door and was about to open it when she took his sleeve. He turned to her and the grotesque face with the cracked red lips and the tooth-gaps was smiling at him.

She nodded her head emphatically and pointed to the 400 he had written on the piece of paper. He waited and, as her smile vanished, she said *"En avance"*. He looked at her, staring blankly, while, exasperated, she stabbed the words on to the paper under the numerals.

Alain read the words and then held up two fingers. She

27

shook her head and held up four. He wagged two at her and she, more vehemently, wagged four. He turned to go.

She grabbed him violently, turned him toward her, and spat at the floor.

"*Eh bien, 200, en avance.*" Her face was twisted, wrinkled and filled with scheming. Baffled by his calm, she sought paper and pencil, testily abandoned the idea, and held up two fingers, nodding and smiling.

Alain turned, walked slowly back to the desk, and fumbled for his money. He had carefully hidden the bulk of his funds and now, from a small packet of rumpled, dirty bills he counted out two hundred francs, made a sign that he wished a receipt, and pushed the money toward the woman on the desk.

She took the money quickly, rushed around behind the counter, placed it in a drawer, and brought out a cheap pad of printed forms. With slashing, jerked strokes she dated the receipt, listed the room number and monthly rate, and then wrote in "200 *francs en avance. Payé*". She copied his name from his identity card, wrote it on a list on the desk, and handed him the key.

Alain de Brielle, OSS operative "O for Zero" had a Paris address.

To anyone familiar with the intricacies of espionage nothing is surprising. For if there is any certainty in this most uncertain of occupations, it is only that nothing is certain. That small detail that seems of little consequence suddenly looms as a terrifying stumbling block. And that which seems almost impossible of attainment is quite simply there for the asking.

Alain's mission was dramatic proof. As a network operative sitting in London, I would have guessed that one of the most difficult single tasks any agent could attempt would be the penetration of the dreaded Gestapo headquarters in Paris.

Alain simply walked in one morning, dully, shyly, and, with his pad and pencil, asked for a job. Janitor, errand boy, cleaner, he would take anything. Somewhat hesitantly he added that he might even consider night work. He wouldn't like it, but he would consider it. Perhaps he would have been thrown out if he had spoken his request, perhaps not. At any rate the guard at the door looked at him with interest, motioned him to wait, and left the room.

A young Nazi lieutenant appeared, started to speak in heavily accented French and then, with slight embarrassment, broke off and began writing. He carried on a running commentary with the guard in German that Alain listened to with apparent unconcern. It emphasized the fact that orders had long since come through to replace military personnel with civilians wherever possible. Manpower was needed at the front. But what the lieutenant was writing was a job offer, to start at once, sweeping and cleaning.

Alain read the note offering the job and nodded his acceptance. The lieutenant smiled, motioned him to follow, and led him into another room. Alain felt his blood suddenly surge when he saw the cameras, the fingerprint equipment, the scales, and the like. The lieutenant spoke to a sergeant. His words were curt, brief, and he turned with a Hitler salute and left the room. The sergeant let him stand unnoticed in the middle of the room, giving him time to firm himself for the ordeal ahead of him, a part of the programme that had taken him completely by surprise. He stood lethargically.

At last the sergeant spoke, and when he got no reaction he came over, took Alain by the arm, and led him to the table where the fingerprinting equipment was assembled. He was talking all the while, a collection of French-German, German-French words, speaking loudly and making gestured commands. Alain reacted as if he heard not a sound. He was fingerprinted. He was photographed, full face and profile.

As he finished with the camera, the sergeant turned and asked him to take off his clothes, got no reaction, tried to gesture and then, impatiently, began to write. He tried a phrase, studied it, crossed it out, and tried again. Then, with a sudden flash of solution, he wrote the single word "Nue" and held it toward Alain. It amused him that the German knew the adjective "naked" with the feminine "e".

With the slow deliberation of an idiot child, Alain took off his clothes. He was then weighed. He was measured. He was examined for scars. And there was special attention as to whether or not he had been circumcised. He was glad he had not been. The sergeant gestured for him to dress, and he put his clothes back on while the sergeant went on with the completion of his papers.

Within the hour he was at work.

He found himself in a jungle of hate, petty jealousies, rivalry, and suspicion. And somehow, among the semi-literate dullards with whom he worked, the fact of his being deaf and dumb only added to the apparent loathing with which they regarded him. There were four others on the cleaning crew: one aged, bent, and ineffective French civilian and three burly, stupid, crude, and sadistic young Nazi enlisted men of the super-race.

Before the week was out they had jumped him. As he went to the basement one day to eat his lunch of bread and cheese, they hit him from behind and knocked him to the cement floor. He fought to rise but, one against three, he never had a chance. They tore at him as if to kill him, choking him, crashing his head against the cement floor, tearing at his face, punching and kicking. Head, back, stomach, groin, they kicked and slashed and beat him until he lost consciousness. Only the unexpected arrival of a couple of off-duty guards broke it up and saved his life.

Alain never knew firsthand how he got back to his room. He only knows that he lay in the hard bed of his small room in the stinking hotel for four days before he was able to get up again and walk. Both eyes were closed, his nose was puffed, his mouth cut. There were bruises on his head, his shoulders, his back. His stomach was so sore he couldn't touch it, and his testicles were swollen to the size of grapefruit, the pain from them extending down his legs and into the pit of his stomach. There was dried blood on the bedding, but someone had removed his clothes and folded them over the chair.

From the old crone who ran the hotel Alain learned that a Nazi truck had brought him home, that he had been carried into the hotel by three German soldiers and placed on his bed. She herself had helped to undress him, had put his clothes over the chair. And she had brought him broth.

He never found out who stole what money he had on his person. And he was grateful for the foresight that had prompted him to hide the bulk of his funds, his radio transmitter, and other equipment back at the little Veyzac farm.

When finally he returned to his job, not really knowing whether or not he still had a job, he found there had been changes. One of the thugs, the ringleader, had been summarily shot as a homicidal psychotic. The other two had been sent to the front for active service. Most surprising of all, Alain was taken to the office of a major who was apparently in charge of the administration of the physical premises and treated almost like a human being. The major showed a real compassion for him, apologized for the "unfortunate incident", and suggested that he might prefer to work on the night shift where he could be alone, polish furniture in the offices of the top command, and do special jobs.

The really productive part of his mission was about to begin.

Alain cultivated the German major. Each night he dusted and polished his desk, shined all the brass, and kept the floor waxed and immaculate. He did this in all of the offices of the top personnel, but he gave special attention to the one contact that had shown him some glimmer of interest.

At first a guard accompanied him into each office as he made his cleaning rounds, sat lolling or reading while he did his work, locked the finished room, and went on to another. There was no attempt at communication, only the silent boredom of the guard, the slow, methodical plodding of the speechless Alain. Sometimes another guard would drop by for conversation with the first, and they talked as if they were alone in the room. After all, the only other person was a deaf-mute, a French one at that, so, they must have reasoned, how could he possibly understand what they were saying?

For the most part their conversation was trivial. It was about sex and the women they had slept with; it was about the boredom of their lives; and there was speculation as to when they might again get leave, any kind of leave, but preferably home leave.

Then it happened. Alain was busily rubbing down the furniture in an office, an office like all the others, desk, chairs, file cabinets, a safe. His guard was seated at the desk reading a paperback book when another guard came in and exclaimed that this, after all, was the room to be in. The money room. His guard grunted agreement, and then the two men began to speculate on how much money there might be in the safe, what kinds of currency were at hand. They vied with each other as to which one had guarded the largest shipments of money to and from this particular room. Alain went on with his work as if nothing had happened, but he had learned an important bit of information. He knew now where to look for the monetary intelligence we wanted. If there was to be any such information it would have to be here. It was up to him to get it.

He studied the room each night. Placement of files and how many. The desk was locked; he had already discovered that by trying to work the drawers as he polished it. The safe—he knew the type, and he was reasonably certain he could work it. He noted windows, heavily hung with blackout curtains. Doors. There was a door to the hall and there was a small communicating door to the next office. That could be useful. His next problem was how to get enough time alone, any time alone in that office.

Human nature and a lot of luck played into his hands. He was working in the major's office, his guard seated at the major's desk eating a sandwich, when the major himself appeared, returned unexpectedly for some late errand. Alain stood up from his floor polishing when he saw the major, but the guard, back to the door, went on with his lunch. The major cut the guard across the shoulders with the military swagger stick that he carried, ordered him to attention and, in loud, angered, sarcastic German, chastised him for the liberties he had taken with the office. When he had finished, he ordered him from the room and told him to report to the Night Officer for disciplinary action. The major then phoned down to the Night Officer and suggested that the guard be punished with a few days' confinement, beginning immediately. There must have been some protestation from the other end about the need for a guard with the cleaner. The major looked toward Alain as he spoke and commented that the deaf-mute was so stupid as to be perfectly safe at large in the building. Alain stood impassively through it all.

The major worked at his desk for a few minutes and then rose. He wrote a note to Alain telling him to go on with his work as usual, that he was very pleased with the attention he had given his office, that he was a reliable employee.

It was difficult to resist the temptation to rifle the files at once. Fortunately, Alain was sophisticated enough at the game to realize that he should go on with his work as usual for a few nights to establish complete confidence. It was a wise decision. Now and then a patrolling guard would pop his head into an office where he was cleaning, grunt, and go on. A whole floor would be unlocked to him, the guards would disappear, and he was on his own.

Several nights later he took his chance. As soon as the floor had been unlocked to him and the guard had left, he went quietly to the money room. For our purposes the files would most likely contain the important information, and he turned to them first. Using a fine piece of wire and a finer touch, he slipped the lock on the first bank of files and began scanning the index. It revealed nothing. At least nothing under money or currency.

He closed the drawer and went quietly to the door to listen for footsteps. His heart was racing now, and he could feel the pressure of the blood raging against his temples. He went back toward the file, wondering in his own mind how the information he sought might be listed, when the word "control" flashed before him. He opened the file again, looked under "control" and found several subtitles from "accident" to "personnel" to "yard". Nothing on money. Nothing on currency. Special. That was a subheading. Special. But then anything could be special. He located the file, pulled it, and gaped at what he saw. Special control was monetary control.

Alain slid the file shut, went again to the door, and peered into the hall. All was quiet. He went quickly back to the file, opened it, and began to read the first communication therein. It was from the head of the *Abwehr* in Berlin, and it suggested that a plan was under consideration for the recall of all five-thousand-franc notes. Opinions and suggestions were being solicited. The plan was still in formation.

Alain closed and locked the file. He had made a mental note of the date of the letter, only two days earlier. It was current information. There was a tremendous feeling of buoyancy in him, and he found it difficult to hold himself down to his patterned dullard's pace. There was enormous excitement in the realization that this was the pay off, this was what all of the endless, tedious, lonely weeks of training, planning, scheming, and dissembling were about. At last he would be doing a job, a real job. The danger involved hardly mattered.

He finished the cleaning of the other offices. He gave them rather special attention in gratitude for his good luck. It was, as usual, six o'clock in the morning when he reported to the guard desk and signed out. He left the building by his usual route, riding his bicycle slowly down the dawn-grey streets only just coming to life. Some three blocks away he changed direction and headed for the small Veyzac farm in the country on the edge of Paris.

It was from there he sent his first message, "Rumour Gestapo recalling all five thousand franc notes. Rumour only. Will check."

He was back at work as usual that night.

It was hardly the glamorous type of spying that the fiction writers and the films delight in creating, Alain's mission. No blondes, no champagne, no crystal chandeliers, no soft music, no love play, no man-about-town bravado for the real espionage agent. That is for the romantics. The real, working, producing spy, the spy whose value is beyond any practical estimate, lives a dedicated, tedious, drab, and terrifyingly lonely existence. And he usually works harder than he has ever worked in his life.

Like Alain. Here was a young man, well born, accustomed to life at its best, educated, travelled, gently mannered, certainly unfamiliar with physical hardship and manual labour. But dedicated and daring beyond the average, he was living like a common drudge, a friendless, unheeded ordinary labourer. As such he had a value to the war effort beyond measure.

The safety, the very life of every OSS agent then operating in France, whether on an espionage or on a sabotage mission, was dependent on the work of this one inconspicuous operative, Alain de Brielle. No single item, no solitary bit of equipment with which an agent is provided, carries such potential danger as his money. More incriminating, more damning, more snaring, more treacherous than any other single factor is the money. Too much is suspect. Too little is constricting. And in a country occupied by an enemy as cunning and ruthless as the Germans, the wrong kind can mean death. There must be no fresh, new notes, pristine from the bank, free of all blemishes. Every serial number, every series, must be checked and rechecked against any "hot" issues.

Alain kept track of it all. From that first message in late October 1943 until he was brought back to London for a few hours of briefing prior to D-Day—it was late March 1944—Alain fed us a continuing and increasingly vital flow of currency intelligence. He checked out the rumour on the five-thousand-franc notes and reported it false. The Germans repeatedly toyed with this idea. There were attempts to set up occupation currencies, as had been done in the Low Countries in the first months of the war, but, fortunately for us, they were discarded as unworkable. There were constant attempts to entrap by the invalidating of a certain series. And there were "area raids" when sudden money searches of shops, individuals, and families occurred. Alain got them all and sent them on to us in time to act, because the German mentality, the German desire for order and plan, found it necessary to advise the Gestapo in Paris of its every move in advance.

Inevitably he was able to pick up other information of value not necessarily connected with our currency operations. All this he sent on. And he even proved himself to be a surprise source of German currency. Once or twice he had been asked by a German if he could change a few marks to francs as a convenience. He had obliged, rather dully and apparently without too close regard for the rate of exchange. Such word passes quickly, and Alain found himself doing a small exchange business quite quietly for the transient personnel at Gestapo headquarters. He signalled us of the fact, and we instructed him to continue the operation. The Germans, I'm sure, thought they had a stupid dupe and a good thing going, making perhaps a franc on every thousand exchanged. But when Alain arrived in London with a large bundle of German money, something we desperately needed and found most difficult to obtain, it gave us great pleasure to think that the much feared Gestapo was helping us to finance our agent operations against them.

He told us how he had worked out the pattern of his operations. His constant use of pencil and paper had been a tremendous factor in helping him with the tedious detail of figures and serial numbers. No one paid any attention to the bits of paper with which his pockets were always stuffed, and he became quite casual in listing pertinent information taken from the files. On his first return visit to the farm to send his message back to use, Alain had taken the Veyzacs into his confidence. They were ready to help in any way, although Marie was worried for his safety, but he impressed upon them the vital fact that they could best help by doing nothing. To live as they had been living would be the best possible cover for him.

Once he had cleaned and dusted and polished the offices on Saturday night, Alain was free until the next Monday night. With this schedule, he was able to leave from work on the Sunday morning, bicycle out to the Veyzac farm, and stay there until Monday afternoon. In this way he could send his messages back to OSS in London on each weekend, provided there was nothing of urgency to report. But when the information was vital, when there was danger in delay, Alain made the trip as soon as possible, often going without sleep for three or four days in a row.

It seems incredible, in retrospect, that he could get away with it as long as he did. And when, at last sitting over a glass of sherry at the Connaught back in London, I expressed my wonderment, Alain was disarmingly amused that I should have found his exploits so amazing. After all, he argued, they accepted him as a deaf and dumb, with emphasis on the dumb, and it had proven, as he had hoped it would, to be a tremendous advantage. He was known as "the dumb one" and much was overlooked and ignored because of that.

He told how he had become more and more trusted by the major. How he had run errands for him, carried messages, and done special cleaning tasks. He told how the major had arranged that he could use the small, inconspicuous table in the corner of the officers' bistro, and he laughed with us at the wonderful incongruity of a German officer buying a drink for and toasting a young Frenchman spying for the OSS in the officers' own Gestapo headquarters. With what I thought monumental understatement, Alain said he had enjoyed the experience.

He told us how he had secreted his radio equipment at the Veyzac farm. With Gustave's help he had ingeniously built a false inner roof to the small shed that housed the swine. The walls of the shed – only three of them, with the fourth side left open to the sun—were made of stone. The wooden rafters supported a roofing of wattles and thatch built to a peak. Alain devised a space under the roof for the sending and receiving of his messages. With old boarding Gustave had at hand, they dropped the inside roof line on one side of the peak by some thirty inches. It allowed only a crawl space but, lying prone, feet braced against the stonework of the wall, Alain was able to operate his radio in relative isolation and security. The swine shed was farthest from the house, his hiding place could be reached only by going in through all the muck and straw of the shelter, and there was the added advantage of the pigs themselves. Their agitated grunts and squeals on being disturbed or approached offered warning to him to stop sending until any danger had passed. As he explained it, there was a soothing factor in hearing the contented grunts and snores beneath him as he worked.

Over the months Alain had become completely familiar

36

with the files in the Monetary Control office at the Paris Gestapo headquarters. Out of that familiarity came much additional information, one snippet of which, I, at least, could have done without. Alain told his bit with a certain satanic glee.

Alain had, one evening, discovered a folder marked: "Special Attention—For Distribution to all Special Intelligence Units, Gestapo, SS, Area Commanders." Inside was a heavy cardboard-covered booklet, loose leaf, containing pages of typewriter-size paper. Each page was a dossier on some special person—biography, career, present assignment, and photograph. Sometimes there were special notations. There were perhaps two dozen pages, and the subjects were American, British, a couple of French, and some Russians. OSS was honoured in the pages with a complete rundown with photograph of General Donovan, the over-all head of the organization; Col. David Bruce, the head of the OSS in the ETO, based in London; Allen Dulles, the OSS chief of mission in Switzerland, later to head the CIA; and, Alain told this with glee, myself.

He told how he read my whole story in Gestapo files. When and where I was born, my education, my study abroad in both England and France, all of my major travels. They had my career as an instructor in a boys' preparatory school and my years as an executive secretary to a Congressman in Washington. They had my war service to date, my rank, and the fact that I was the man handling all the financing of espionage and sabotage operations for the Office of Strategic Services from the Baltic to the Mediterranean. There was a listing of physical characteristics, height, weight, colouring and the like. Alain said there was a very good photograph of me, in uniform, smiling and carefree as a schoolboy that appeared to have been taken on Grosvenor Street in London.

This was shattering information to one who somehow naïvely thought that no one in the world other than his direct superiors in the OSS had any idea of what he was doing. There was worse.

In large, black letters across the bottom of the page and underlined with a black line were the words, in German of course, "TO BE TAKEN ALIVE".

I can't honestly say, knowing what I did of Gestapo torture methods, that I found the notation especially comforting. Nor did I find any real satisfaction in the knowledge that my own office had a similar dossier on the opposite numbers in the German, Italian, and Japanese services.

There was one more thing I wanted to know from Alain. I wanted to know how he had got himself excused from his job for the few days necessary to return to London. We had sent him word that we would like him to come back for a short briefing, that he was to work out his own time schedule and advise us when to pick him up. He would be lifted from the same country field at which he had first landed.

In the telling of it now it sounds as simple as going down to the travel office and booking a seat for a given flight. It was infinitely more complex. It called for almost split-second timing involving many different persons; it called for the ultimate in secrecy; and it called for courage and daring of magnificent proportions. To get Alain out of France for his few hours of briefing, it was necessary for our London base to alert, by clandestine radio, the resistance workers operating for us at the designated field. Once Alain had picked his date and notified us, we cleared with the field personnel in France and the pilot and crew in England. Exact details had to be worked out: exact time of arrival of the plane in France; departure time (only a few minutes after arrival, for obvious reasons); whether or not a second pass at the field would be tried in case the first attempt aborted; an alternate date should weather or other factors make the original plan impossible. All this had to be set up ahead of time. It made it most difficult for an agent working openly in a job with the enemy to find a pretext for being absent, and it was this one factor in Alain's assignment that was perhaps the weakest point and therefore potentially the most dangerous. An agent operating constantly undercover has a freedom of movement denied to one holding a set job. And when that job happens to be in the middle of the enemy camp, the restrictions are obvious, the dangers innumerable.

Alain recognized all of this. He could not feign illness for two reasons: first, he had to give us enough notice of an exact date to make the necessary arrangements for the lift; and second, he left himself wide open for failure either through refusal of sick leave or discovery of his deception. Alain took the only course open to him. He went to the major who had placed so much confidence in him and asked, quite simply and somewhat shyly, if he might have a few days off to visit his family. Four days, five at the most, and he would see that his job was covered by a substitute.

The German major watched him closely as Alain wrote his request and explained his arrangements. He frowned as he read the note, tapped it against his fingers, and then took a pencil from his desk. When he handed the paper back to Alain he had written, in schoolboy French, that he could have six days, but they would be at half-pay. He smiled as he saw Alain's reaction. Then he reached in a drawer, drew out a small pad of pale blue forms and wrote one out, signing it with a quickly scratched signature, underlined. It was a Gestapo pass to help Alain through any road blocks or police inspections!

Alain showed it to me with great pride. He had forty-eight hours in London. We got his whole story. We gave him additional briefings on things to look for. We fed him well, he went to the theatre, and he went nightclubbing. And then, almost as nonchalantly as one would take the 8.05 into Grand Central, he boarded his plane and left for the second lap of his assignment.

Thirty-six hours later he was back scrubbing floors, polishing desks and, incidentally, scanning files at Gestapo headquarters in Paris.

April, May, . . . JUNE. D-DAY.

Alain fed us a constant stream of high-level intelligence, not only on currency matters, but of every description. He reported the consternation among the German personnel where he worked over the monumental force of the Allied landings. And there was a kind of staccato brevity to his messages that somehow indicated his growing excitement over the progress of the Allied troops.

His last message came through on 17th June. It concerned more efforts at currency control; it told of rising tension at Gestapo headquarters and that severe measures for the control of the Parisian populace were under consideration; that spot arrests were being stepped up in an effort to terrorize anyone with Allied sympathies.

Then there was silence.

One is never ready for it. One knows, at the start of every espionage or sabotage mission, that there can be losses, that some are bound to fail. But one is never ready. Three or four days without a message, even a week, that may be routine, and one accepts. A quick stab of uneasy alarm, but acceptance nonetheless. Then there are eight, nine, ten days without a word. One is worrying now, but one takes the consoling way out and guesses that there must have been nothing to report. Eleven, twelve, thirteen, fourteen days. One curses the fact that there is no way to make contact, that all communication in this type of operation depends on agent contacting base. Now there is real alarm, a dread that must be covered lest it infect the others operating around one. This is the period of wild surmises, of imaginings when one tries the most improbable explanations for the silence, anything but the real one, the one already known deep down but not acknowledged. Perhaps he is "hot" and is in hiding for a while—and yet one knows that for Alain to go into hiding would mean a warning to the Gestapo that something was wrong. It would mean the end of his mission.

There was one last possible explanation, the D-F-ers, the direction-finder boys. These were the radio snoopers who operated from mobile units beamed in to sniff out clandestine radio transmitters. They were the nightmare threat to every agent operating a hidden radio and called for constant vigilance, often constant change of operating base, to avoid detection. If Alain's radio message from the Veyzac farm had been picked up by the Germans, not yet pinpointed but known to exist, he would be in danger, and it would be necessary for him to cease sending for a while or to change his hidden base. It was the only possible explanation one could accept other than the final one. It was a consoling explanation, and one accepts it for a while. But only for a while.

Then, after days became weeks, after Paris was liberated and there was still no word of Alain, one is forced to accept what one has refused to see, refused to admit. There is the horrible, weakening, dulling, self-critical realization that our agent is lost.

It was autumn in 1945 when I finally found Marie and Gustave Veyzac. Although I was not familiar with the town or the area in which they lived, I knew from Alain where to find them. And yet, on the kind of mission that would bring me to the Veyzac farm, one did not move blindly or too openly to make contact.

40

This may sound strange to anyone who did not know France immediately after the war. And it brings up a particularly unattractive era in the modern history of France. Suspicion was everywhere, an evil so overwhelming at times as to be almost tactile. Accusations, recriminations, revenge, hatred, jealousy, everything was whispered, anything was rumoured, and nothing could be believed. *Collaborateurs!* That was the cry of every and any Frenchman who had a private grudge against another Frenchman. *Résistance!* That was the cry of every Frenchman who hoped to gain honour, a fleeting hero worship, perhaps money. To have been a resistance worker could mean one or all. Claims, accusations, threats, and denials, France was a seething morass of suspicion.

It made my own job especially difficult. Obviously there were many loyal Frenchmen and women whom the OSS had relied on for massive aid. They had existed in the midst of danger, treachery, and cunning throughout the war, often exhibiting greater courage and daring than many a front-line soldier. They asked nothing in return. They worked selflessly and anonymously for the liberation of France. It was the feeling on the part of the OSS that they should, wherever possible, be given some tangible evidence of our good faith. It was my job to see that they got it.

It called for discretion. It called for a certain amount of secrecy. It called for honest appraisal of the job done. And because of the climate of suspicion, the chance for revenge or monetary gain, it called for a monumental sifting of claims and counter-claims in many cases. We did everything possible to keep our contact with these people unknown to their neighbours, their friends, and even their relatives in order to spare them unnecessary attention or possible unpleasantness.

Using ordinary notepaper so as not to arouse the interest of even the postman in the little village where they lived, I wrote a note to Marie and Gustave Veyzac. In it I told them briefly that, as a friend of Alain de Brielle, I should like to meet and talk with them. I asked if it would be advisable for me to come to their farm or whether they would prefer a meeting elsewhere. A note came back to me in Paris, very correct and formal, saying that they would like very much to have me come to the farm. They added that Alain had spoken often of me so they felt we were already friends. The use of the past tense in speaking of Alain skewered me with a sudden pain of truth. It was the first proof that he was dead.

I arrived at the Veyzac farm in mid-afternoon. It was a grey-gold autumn day when the sun seemed to have lost interest in shining and only cast a suggestion of light over the dull haze that pervaded everything. Some hedgerows and trees were still in leaf, some almost green, but for the most part the foliage was browning and sparse. Marie Veyzac had given explicit directions for reaching their farm, but I would not have needed them. It was just as Alain had described it with the perceptive eye of a good agent. There was the rutted lane, the hedgerows, the orchard, the grey stone house hitched to the larger, dominant stone barn, the outbuildings. A thin twist of smoke came from one of the chimneys of the house and mingled with the grey-gold of the haze. Chickens scattered before the car, and a flock of geese waddled away with honking distress, undecided as to whether or not to abandon dignity altogether and run for it. They waddled instead, only faster.

Both Marie and Gustave came out to meet me. She was dressed in the inevitable black, quite obviously her Sunday dress, and she wore a stiff white apron with much embroidery and peepholes in it. Her hair was snow-white and twisted into a knot at the back of her head, her cheeks were full and pink, and her eyes were dark, warm, and sad. She was short and plump. Gustave was only a trifle taller. His hair still held some of the original dark, and his eyebrows and moustache, long and ragged, were almost black. He had a large, straight, firm nose, and his eyes were clear, dark, and penetrating. He gave the impression of being slightly younger than Marie, though they both were well into their sixties.

We went through the kitchen. It was moist-warm with a boiling tea-kettle spouting steam and a huge black kettle on the back of the stove simmering and steaming and giving out wonderful odours of *pot-au-feu*. There was a fire in the fireplace of the small sitting room, there was a table laid with a lace cloth, and there were glasses, decanters of wine, teacups, saucers, and plates, and there were cakes, home-made bread, home-made butter, jams, and fruit, all the abundance of a farm. It made the war seem ages past, though just outside and at every turn was the destruction and desolation it had brought.

They told me what they knew of Alain.

Alain had been an absolutely first-class agent. How good was borne out by the fact that Marie and Gustave Veyzac really knew so very little of the work he was doing. For their protection as well as his own, it was apparent to Alain that they should know as little as possible. This is perhaps the most basic rule of espionage, that every contact made by an agent should know only the barest minimum essential to his own function in an operation. The Veyzacs, for instance, did not know that Alain had been in England after the fall of France, and they were stunned when I told them that we had dropped him into France by parachute, taken him out for a briefing in London, and then dropped him again to continue his mission.

They had suspected, but they did not know for sure until I confirmed the fact, that Alain was actually operating in Paris. This he had withheld from them. And yet, in some detail and in contrast to his highly developed sense of security, he had told them what had happened. Why? Perhaps because he had to get the horror out of his system. Perhaps because he felt that he would surely be caught and he wanted someone to know what had gone wrong. Perhaps he hoped that I would some day know.

As Marie told her story in her slow, quiet voice, filled with sadness, Alain had arrived one morning toward the end of June. He had been coming frequently for several days, stopping with them only long enough to have a bite to eat and exchange news bits. Then he would crawl into his hidden retreat in the roof of the swine shed and send his messages. By now both Marie and Gustave knew that Alain was operating as an agent for the Allied forces, that he had a clandestine radio transmitter in the swine shed, and that he was increasingly excited over the landings and the progress of the war. But they asked no questions and were only ready to assist him if help should be needed.

They had told him, shortly after D-Day, that there was increased military activity on the part of the Germans in their area. They were not on the direct line of advance from the beach-heads to Paris but they were close enough to the main routes to feel the new tensions, the new pressures, building up around them. The increasing excitement of the people over the Allied assault was offset by increased terrorist activities on the part of the Germans. One farmer they knew had had his hands chopped off because he clung to his bicycle when

43

the Germans decided to requisition it. Another, a neighbour, had been forced to watch a group of the master race rape his wife and ten-year-old daughter. And when they had finished with them they turned to him, stripped him of his clothes, circumcised him with a pocketknife, and then laughingly cut *"Jude"* across his chest with the same blade. They left him, streaming blood, tied to a tree, his wife and child too hysterical to aid him. The fortunate ones had only had their homes looted and then burned.

These things they had told Alain, and he had cursed the Nazi swine. He showed no apprehension, no haunted worry, until that particular morning. Marie remarked that he seemed uneasy as they ate an ample country lunch. He stayed in the house throughout the afternoon, not going near his radio transmitter, and then, that evening, after they had had supper, he told them what had happened.

Without mentioning Gestapo headquarters, Alain told them that he had had access to a great deal of important information about the Germans, their plans, their estimates of success, their gains and losses—vital information. One room in particular held these secrets. Since the Allied landing, there had been an absolute flood of correspondence, orders, counter-orders, defensive and offensive plans, the like. He was being swamped with material, and he was having to be selective. To do that he had to scan, at least, almost everything available and then make notes on the important and urgent material. That room, we know (but the Veyzacs did not), was the "money room" he had so rewardingly penetrated at Gestapo headquarters.

He had done his perfunctory cleaning and polishing. This he still had to do to keep his cover intact and to avoid suspicion. But as quickly as possible he had gone to the room to open the files. For weeks now he had taken the precaution to open the door to the adjoining room in the hope that he might, if surprised at work, pretend to dust and polish himself into the next room. The principal files were luckily standing next to the intercommunicating door, and he had long since thought out a method whereby he could appear to be working through the doorway if someone should suprise him at the files.

The very surfeit of the information available was his undoing. Carefully he had selected the most recent communications, closed the file drawer and, seated on the floor to the side

44

of the file cabinet, was winnowing the material. He made notes as he went along on the tiny pad he carried, cryptic shorthand notes that only he could decipher. He was working intensely and quickly. He had finished one file, replaced it, taken another, and closed the drawer. He went quietly to the door, peered into the hall, and listened. Nothing. No one. No sound. He glanced at his watch. It was ten minutes past three in the morning. Less than three hours to cull the files. It would be difficult to do at a steady, concentrated pace. Having constantly to be on the alert, stopping to listen, to check, made the task tedious and dangerous.

His mops, brooms, polishes, and cloths were beside him as he started making notes on the next file. There was much of importance, and he became completely absorbed in his material —so absorbed he never heard the footsteps untl they were just outside the door, coming on rapidly, coming in. There was no time to get the material back to the file, no time to do more than slide it behind the cabinet, grab a dustcloth and go on with his work. Bent over, cleaning the base of a table, he could hear and only partially see the figure of a guard as he came into the room. The grey trousers, the black boots, they were there, in the doorway. Alain kept on working, seeming not to hear, seeming unaware of the guard's presence. The role of the deaf-mute had its advantages, though his heart was pounding, his face felt flushed, and he could already feel the cold rivulets of sweat chilling his back.

The guard spoke a few words in German. Alain ignored him. He raised his voice, this time in broken French. Alain went on with his dusting. The guard strode across the room and with a brutal thrust of his heavy boot kicked Alain on the buttocks and sent him sprawling against the file cabinet. Alain got up and stood facing the guard. The guard wasn't looking at him and Alain followed his gaze. He was staring at the file cabinet, one of the drawers jarred slightly forward by the impact of Alain's body. Without a word the guard stepped forward and tried the other drawers of the file, found them all unlocked, and slid them back and forth a couple of times while Alain watched him dumbly. In another second he had wheeled with his gun drawn, pointed menacingly at Alain.

Alain shrugged his shoulders and stood as if dully uncomprehending, hoping the ruse would work, counting on his feigned dullness and stupidity to save him. The German held his gun on him and then, as if confused by the situation, not knowing how to communicate, hesitated, spoke again in German and motioned toward the files with his gun. Alain shrugged again. The German, exasperated, turned toward the desk, put down his gun, and reached for paper and pencil. The action brought his eyes in line with the base of the file cabinet and the tell-tale edge of the file Alain had stuffed behind it. He straightened up, looking piercingly at the partially hidden file and knelt forward to pick it up.

Alain acted. As the German leaned toward the file, Alain lunged his full weight on to his back, pinning him to the floor. At the same moment he had twisted his cleaning cloth, knotted around the guard's neck, tighter, tighter, tighter, until his fingers ached with the strain. There was a violent, tensing, hardening struggle under him, there was a muffled groan, a kind of escaping of air, a gradual softening and relaxing of the body, a twitch. Alain tightened the roped cloth. Perspiration was starting on his forehead, but he dared not relax his grip until he was sure. Then, like a tyre suddenly gone flat, there was a spasm, he felt the German's body let go, and he was dead.

Alain moved quickly. He slipped the knotted cloth from around the guard's neck, shook it out, and stuffed it into the pocket of his work smock. He took the file folder from behind the cabinet, placed it back in the drawer, and locked the file. He went to the door into the hall, listened for a moment, and then peered into the hall. All was still. He went back to the room, checked the files and the safe again to make sure they were secure, and then lifted the German's gun from the desk where he had left it. Carefully, rubbing his fingerprints from the gun and using a cloth, he slipped the gun back into the holster buckled to the dead guard's side. He dusted over the furniture again, checked every detail of the room to make sure all was in order, and then put out the lights. He slipped the night lock on the door into the hall and closed it from the inside. Then, going through the communicating door to the next office, he locked that behind him. He had all of his cleaning materials with him and he went on down the hall, closing and locking the doors, putting out lights, until most of the building was in darkness.

He went into another room far down the hall from the one in which he had left the dead guard and began his cleaning.

His instinct told him to run, to flee for his life and, as he told the Veyzacs, the physical compulsion to run—somewhere, anywhere, but run—was almost too powerful to resist. His agent's training told him to stay, to do everything possible to keep the routine, to avoid suspicion.

This is where the tempered-steel courage of the really top agent asserts itself. It is not bravado, not the heroics of a grandstand play, not boastful overconfidence. That is the way to discovery and death. This kind of bravery is cool and calculating, scheming and planned. It calls for nerve, nerve, and then more nerve.

Alain had it. Quietly, as he went on with his cleaning, he assessed his situation, studied the various courses of action open to him, and decided to take the long chance. It was impossible to leave the building without signing out at the guard's desk. To leave early would call for explanation, explanation would arouse suspicion, and as soon as the body of the guard was discovered he, if he had left early, would be the prime suspect. With the nerve to brazen it out and stay through his full work period, he could, with luck, divert that first suspicion. He took the gamble.

It seemed as if six o'clock would never come. Never had it been more difficult to play the part of the deaf-mute. Every sound, every shadow, carried its own implied menace, and he fought against his mounting tension. And succeeded. For when he finally appeared at the guard's desk to sign out, shuffling slowly, head down as usual, hands in pockets, the guard only pushed the sign-out book at him without looking up, grunted as he passed it back, and went on with his papers.

Alain mounted his bicycle and rode slowly down the street. And here he had made another crucial decision. His first impulse had been to disappear quickly into the country and hide out at the Veyzac farm. His pride as an agent, his personal, calm courage argued against it. To disappear would be an admission of guilt, he would be sought out in every nook and cranny of France by the dread Gestapo, his mission would be over. He knew the importance of the material to which he had access. His sense of duty told him that he should cling to everything, anything, that would permit him to continue his assignment.

He rode slowly back to the dirty, dreary hotel where he lived.

Alain left his bicycle in a small shed at the back of the hotel. He had arranged for this soon after he had taken up residence, and it had two attractive features. It was a more protected place to keep it. It was located almost directly under the one small window to the room that he occupied. He padlocked it to a length of chain set into the stonework of the building and then, through the rear entrance of the hotel, went to his room. He saw no one.

He was calmer now. The bicycle ride through the city in the early morning had cleared his brain and he felt almost relaxed, certainly tired, as he took off his clothes and got ready for bed. He stood for a moment watching the growing daylight from the window and then climbed into bed. At first the terror of the night played itself out before his closed eyes, behind his lids, until he thought he would never again be able to sleep. Then, at last, he slept soundly.

He heard the voices, coming closer, getting louder, before he heard the knock on the door. Wide-awake in an instant, he glanced at his watch to find it was a little after three in the afternoon. There was excited French, broken French with a German accent, then the scratching and rattling of a key in the door, and they were there. The old crone, still holding the master key in her hand, was talking excitedly and loudly. She was explaining and apologizing for the intrusion, saying that the officer had insisted that he had urgent business with him; that as a deaf-mute he of course could not hear a knock, so would he pardon, please, the intrusion. Alain lay inert, unheeding, apparently unhearing.

He then heard the German voice, the badly spoken French explaining that a private interview of the utmost importance was necessary, thank you very much, Madame, and that he would stop by at the office when he left. He wished no interruption. It was the German major's voice, but Alain only looked at him, then at the old woman, and waited. There was a sudden embarrassed exchange of polite formalities, much bowing and smiling, and the old woman backed out of the door and closed it firmly with a loud click.

Alain started to get out of bed as the major came toward him, but the German motioned to him to stay as he was. He drew up the only chair in the room next to the bed, took out a pad and pencil, and began to write. He wrote for a long time in silence, crossing out and rewriting a word here and there in

48

his schoolboy French. There was a strained, serious look in his eyes as he handed the note to Alain, and he watched intently as Alain read.

The note said a guard had been found dead in one of the rooms at the headquarters building. It was a strange thing. there seemed to be no motive, no struggle, it was a death by strangulation. Everyone was being questioned (the "everyone" was underlined). The major said he had volunteered to interview Alain because he was interested in him and had confidence in him.

Alain tried to react with suitable expressions as he read. Then at the bottom of the page he wrote asking the name of the guard, where he was found, and when. The answers were duly jotted down for him, and in reply he wrote that he had seen the guard only once that evening—when he reported in for work.

A decided look of relief came over the major's face, and his whole manner changed. He took a fresh piece of notepaper and suggested that perhaps Alain would like to dress and come over to his apartment. It was pleasanter, cosier, and he was sure the furniture was softer.

There was a strange, hungering, searching look in his eyes, and as Alain was reading the note the major leaned forward, slid one hand under the covers, and reached for his leg.

Alain's reaction was reflex. With one forward lunge of his body from a half-reclining position he was out of bed and at the major's throat. There was a half-strangled, half-pleading cry of "Nein, nein". There was a terrified look of the eyes, disbelieving, glazed, and then the German, half the size of Alain, fell before him without the slightest resistance. When his fury had subsided, there was only a rumpled grey uniform looking grotesquely stuffed into human form. The eyes were staring and glazed, the swollen tongue protruded from a corner of the mouth, and there was a trace of foamed saliva glistening on the chin. Only this to indicate that here had been life only seconds before.

Alain dressed quickly.

He listened at the door to the hall for a moment. Crossing the room he raised the shade, gently. He worked the metal fasteners that closed the casement window, opened it slowly, and peered out. The rear courtyard was deserted. In another moment he had slid from the window to the roof of the small shed and then to the ground. He unlocked the padlock that secured his bicycle, tossed the chain aside, and rolled the cycle out of the courtyard into the narrow alley. A few paces down the street two women in shawls, laden with bundles, were walking away from him, unaware of his presence. Alain mounted his bicycle and rode quickly off in the opposite direction.

Alain's cunning, the shrewdness, the ability to calculate and appraise the risks the principal factors that made him such an outstanding agent—are all highlighted by his next moves. He left Paris by a completely different route from the one he usually used to reach the Veyzac farm, on the slight chance that he might be followed. And somewhere along the way he made a major decision to throw any pursuers off the scent. He discarded his role as a deaf-mute.

There was a Nazi checkpoint on all the roads leading out of the city, and he well knew that his exit and direction would be recalled, once the alert had gone out. He still had the pale-blue Gestapo pass given him by the major, but it noted that he was a deaf-mute. To use it now, although it would ease his way through, would be to spotlight his passing, once all areas had been signalled to watch for and arrest a deaf-mute of such description. All of his papers were in order, and he decided to take his chances.

He could see the barrier ahead, the red-and-white-striped bar across the highway to impede traffic, the wire gate for the pedestrians, the privy-like guard boxes. It was a busy time of day, and there were many others there, coming in and going out, and he took his place in line. He had dismounted from his bicycle, and he had his papers ready, his identity card between his teeth, his work card in his hand. He fought his nervousness as the guard reached for his papers, scanned them, and handed them back. He hardly glanced at him.

"*Danke.*"

"*Danke.*" And he was on his way.

The route he had chosen to the Veyzacs was much longer than his usual one, and he spent the night hidden in a hedge-row in a remote country lane. It was mid-morning when he reached the Veyzac farm.

It was typical of Alain that he should be more worried for the Veyzacs than for himself. Carefully he explained to them the danger. As soon as the major's body was discovered, there would be an alert out for him. The Gestapo would spare nothing, no one, in its search for "the dumb one". They had his fingerprints, his physical characteristics—his age, height, weight, colouring. Only one thing could possibly save him— they would be broadcasting an alert for a deaf-mute, a deaf-mute who did not exist. But the Gestapo had well earned its dread reputation; it was ruthless, thorough, cunning, and persistent. They could, in time, trace him to the Veyzac farm.

He was sure of one thing. There was no suspicion, there could be no suspicion of him as an enemy agent. He had left no trace of his operations, not a clue to show the magnificent deception he had carried on for so many months. And he cursed himself for the blunders that had suddenly ended his usefulness as an agent. He would, he said, with the Veyzacs' permission, stay on there for a few days. He would stay in hiding. Then, when he felt it was safe, he wanted to contact London, send in his last intelligence material from the Gestapo, and seek further work in the field.

Marie told of those last few days. Alain kept to the house entirely or hid in the roof of the swine shed. He was anxious lest some of the Veyzacs' neighbours, some of the villagers, would learn of his presence and spread the word that there was a young man staying at the farm. He knew very well that innocent neighbourhood gossip can be lethal for any agent. For an agent in hiding, it is death.

Then, one evening when he could no longer endure the inactivity and the boredom, he assisted Gustave with the chores. It was a glorious, warming June night, late in coming, and he lingered outside breathing in of the moist warmth of the farm smells, the earth, the grass, the flowers, the animals, a potpourri of sensual delights. He was about to go into the house when the glaring headlights of a motor vehicle shone at the end of the lane. Alain never went into the house. Instead he turned and ran for the swine shed and crawled into his hiding place.

The car growled slowly down the farm lane and stopped at the door. It was a German command car, and there were four Nazis in uniform seated in it. One of them came to the door and knocked heavily and was about to open the door when Gustave appeared before him. The German pushed himself into the house while the three others got out of the car and followed him.

Marie was in the kitchen, and when they saw her the Nazis took off their caps and softened their belligerence. It didn't last long.

They began their questions. How many were there in the family? Only two? Why no children? What did they raise? How many hectares? How many buildings? How many cattle? Horses? Sheep? Pigs? What of poultry? The questions were pelted at them.

Marie and Gustave answered them all. It was not the first time they had been visited by the Nazis and harassed with unnecessary and insolent questions.

While one of the Nazis continued the questioning, the other three wandered the house from room to room, from top to bottom, peering into everything, probing and searching. They finally came back to the kitchen, and the questioning became uglier.

Where was the young man who had been seen in the farmyard that evening? There was a young man. He had been seen. Where was he?

Marie and Gustave knew of no young man. The questioner muttered to the other three, and they fled out of the kitchen and started across the barnyard. They took huge flashlights with them and went through the barn, the poultry house, the sheepfold, the swine shed.

When they came back to the kitchen they reported that they had found nothing.

Marie concealed her relief by commenting that she wasn't surprised, as there was no one to find. Her comment was met with glaring silence.

The Nazis announced that they would stay the night at the Veyzac farm, that they would search the place more thoroughly in the daylight, that they would stay until they had found the young man they knew must be hiding there.

The battle of nerves began. Fortunately Alain had long since worked out a code for just such an emergency. He had absolutely no way of knowing, from his hiding place in the roof of the swine shed, what was going on around him, who might be at the farm, whether or not it would be safe to appear. Therefore he had worked out with Marie and Gustave a simple code. If there was danger, either Marie or Gustave would call the family cat three times. Three times only. What more natural action in a farm household than to stand at the kitchen door and call the cat? Three such calls, and Alain was to stay hidden until either Marie or Gustave walked past the swine shed and gave the "all clear".

It was past midnight when, fed on *pot-au-feu*, bread, cheese, and wine, the four Nazis arranged the schedule of their watch. Two would stay on watch for four hours while the other two slept, and vice versa. They had no intention of permitting the Veyzacs to be left alone or out of sight. And while they were arranging the details of their schedule, Marie Veyzac stood just outside the kitchen door with a saucer of milk and called the cat. Once. Twice. A third time her voice shrilled in the night air. Then, setting the saucer by the step, she came inside, closed the door, and began settling the house as she had done every night of her life—as if nothing had happened.

The four Nazis were out early the next morning. They asked for and got hearty breakfasts of eggs and bacon and hot breads. Marie, hate and fear churning inside her in a wild maelstrom, treated them with quiet civility. Two of the men stayed with Gustave while he did his chores, and the other two stayed with Marie. Then, when Gustave had finished the tending of his animals, the two men insisted that they would, with him, search every corner of the farm. Marie, casually called the cat again and went on with her own chores in the house.

The Nazis were thorough. They went completely through the house again. They went through the huge stone barn, the feed bins, the hay mows, the tool sheds, the small dairy room. They opened every door, prodded every bale and bag in the sheepfold and the poultry house. But they were not thorough enough. They simply walked around the three solid sides of the swine shed, peered into the open side, commented on the muck and the size of the hogs, and went on.

They walked the fields with Gustave. They peered into the drainage ditches. They thrust bayonets into the hedgerows. But they found nothing. They were surly, sullen, and irritable at the evening meal and announced that they would stay that night and all the next day and night. That they would, in fact, stay until they found the young man they knew was in hiding there. Or else burn the buildings down around them.

Marie and Gustave, inwardly alarmed, listened impassively.

And when the evening meal was over, Marie went again to the door with a saucer of milk and called the cat three times. Her voice was higher pitched than usual, but in no other way did she betray her concern.

The next morning, quite abruptly, after breakfast, the four Nazis announced that they were leaving. They were now all courtesy and forced politeness. They thanked Madame and Monsieur for their hospitality. They were sorry for the inconvenience. It was all a misunderstanding.

Their car grumbled down the rutted farm lane.

Gustave and Marie watched them go. Waited until they had reached the road at the end of the lane. And suddenly it was more nerve-racking, more shattering somehow with the Nazis gone. The Veyzacs were familiar with Nazi tactics. Too many of their friends and neighbours had felt the sting and tragedy of Nazi treachery for them to feel that their ordeal was over. Too often had they heard of this particular ruse. The long, nerve-straining Nazi grilling and search, the sudden departure, the huge relief of deliverance, the reappearance and rejoicing of the hidden quarry. Then, the sudden reappearance of the Nazi bullyboys, the tortures, and the killings.

Her heart filled with worry and fear, her thoughts constantly on Alain unfed, cramped, perhaps suffocating in his hiding place, Marie Veyzac steeled herself against her softer impulses. Once again she went to the kitchen door and called three times for her cat.

Gustave went on with his chores, his daily routine. And yet he felt as if every move he made, everything he did, might somehow be scrutinized from afar by the hated Germans.

Then it happened.

About lunchtime three trucks teetered and bumped down the farm lane. They were filled with German troops, steel-helmeted men armed with rifles and machine guns, and almost before the trucks had stopped, the men were out and swarming over the farm. A burly officer was shouting orders, and somehow platoons formed and another search began. Through the house they swarmed, tracking in mud and filth, knocking over furniture, pocketing trinkets from the little rooms.

Marie and Gustave were taken out into the yard and made to strip. When naked, their hands were tied behind their backs and then they were roped together, back to back, two ageing, harmless, kindly countrypeople, degraded and humiliated. One soldier made much sport of lifting Marie's ample breasts with the point of his bayonet, and when his comrades responded with ribald and mocking laughter, he was encouraged to lower the bayonet and commit further probing indecencies. They turned their attention to Gustave, poked and prodded him with their bayonets, shaved at his pubic hair with the razor edge of the blade, and threatened to castrate him.

Several of the men concentrated on the kitchen, ate everything in sight, bread, cheese, eggs, milk, and emptied the huge kettle of steaming country soup. Marie discovered later that they had urinated into the huge kettle as a final insult.

The officer in charge made little effort to curb the cruelties and insults. He seemed rather to encourage them deliberately to intimidate, terrorize, and insult the two helpless Veyzacs, stopping the perverted carnival only to send the men further afield in search of the whole farm area.

They overran the farm buildings. Some, with bayonets fixed, charged hay bales, grain sacks, feed bins, anything that might conceivably offer concealment. Fortunately the cattle were all at pasture, as were the sheep and two of the horses. Two other horses and the herd bull and the swine, still penned, were cut down with machine guns. The chickens and geese were blown to gusts of bloody feathers.

There were two huge haystacks just on the edge of the main pasture. These the Nazis riddled with machine-gun fire and then calmly set ablaze. The house and the attached huge barn, all of stone with tile roofs, were not tempting for this kind of treatment. But the men soon discovered that they could cut patterns in the roofs with machine-gun bullets. At first it was aimless, and then, with concentration, they tried cutting an enormous swastika in the roof of the barn with rattling bursts of the machine guns.

And then, while Marie and Gustave watched in helpless horror, they turned to the other buildings. They riddled the roof of the sheepfold. They cut and shredded the roof of the poultry house, and they zigzagged up and down and across the roof of the swine shed. Then, almost as an afterthought, one Nazi forked a tuft of burning hay from one of the stacks and tossed it on to the roof of the swine shed. In an instant the dry thatch and wattles were a flaming mass, sending off huge clouds of black smoke.

Marie lost consciousness. Gustave felt her slump against his back, and when he spoke to her there was no answer, only a sobbing, and then a heavy, erratic breathing.

Neither of them could remember how long this hell had lasted. But end it did. And when the soldiers of the master race had finally been herded back into the trucks, their pockets bulging with all kinds of loot, and the trucks had pulled slowly out the narrow lane, Marie and Gustave Veyzac were left alone with the shambles of their farm.

Somehow Gustave got them untied, and he carried Marie, now only half conscious and semi-hysterical, into the house. He put her gently into bed, gave her cognac, and brought a cool towel for her brow. Then, desperately, sadly, Gustave dressed and went out to wander the debris of his farm.

Past the great barn, deathly still, the huge bulk of the horses and the bull in their stalls, still bleeding. Past the shattered sheepfold, past the riddled poultry house. The roof of the swine shed had fallen in and was still smouldering, though the dry thatch and wattles had burned to a white ash. Gustave made himself go on. There, in the burned-out muck of the hogpen, lay Alain's sprawled body. It had been shredded with machine-gun fire. It was charred beyond recognition.

The remains of his transmitter lay twisted nearby.

Alain de Brielle, had he not impetuously killed the German major, might have lived to write his own story. It was the unexpected flaw, the sudden, irrational, disastrous action in an otherwise spectacular espionage performance.

He was an agent, cool, controlled, disciplined to the ultimate. He was able to live and pose as a deaf-mute for months in the very midst of the enemy, to brazen out the killing of a guard on the reasoned assurance that it would be his best protection, and yet he had broken on impulse against the German major's advance.

General Donovan discussed it with me on several occasions long after the war was over. It was his feeling that something in the major's manner or attitude indicated to Alain that he was suspect, that his only hope for escape from the charge of killing the guard was either submission to the major or the course he chose. The General felt that Alain was too perceptive to have missed the point. He felt that Alain knew that the major was only leading him into a trap, a trap that would have led him into the torture clutches of the Gestapo.

The only other explanation would have been sudden blind panic or nerves brought on by the experience of killing the guard, the strain of staying through the night to finish his work, and then the confrontation with the major. A weaker man would certainly have broken, and yet everything about Alain's mission up to that point had been brilliant in its courage and sophistication.

We will never know. Tension? Miscalculation? Calculated risk? Hate? Panic? Any one could be the explanation, could have triggered the action.

CHAPTER TWO

GINA

THERE are endless nightmares of uncertainty in the running of an espionage and sabotage organization. And they are not all concerned with the agent himself. He, of course, has the immediate, constant, ever threatening danger of discovery, torture, and death. With all of these he must live, his survival and success dependent upon himself alone, once he is operating in enemy territory. The tensions, the nerve strain and fatigue, the all-demanding alertness of living a lie, these are his to meet, accept, and control. They are never, really, conquered. They are always there, part of the occupational hazards of being a spy.

But there are tensions back at the operating base that are just as frightening and of vastly important implications. Though it is never put into words, never openly acknowledged, the agent and his base operating officer are always aware that capture and death can come at any time. What is brutal to admit is the fact that the death of an agent can be accepted. And provided his death has not uncovered his mode of operation or his contacts in the field, the damage can be repaired in time. Provided the security has been maintained, the over-all effectiveness of the network continues.

However, there is one haunting, terrifying, nightmare possibility that pervades the thinking of anyone occupied with running an agent. That is the threat of the "double agent". The Office of Strategic Services utilized only volunteers as agents in the field, and they were as rigidly trained, carefully screened, security-checked, and watchfully guarded as any such volatile group could be. And they were well paid. From the very earliest use of spies in modern intelligence work, several centuries ago, it was an accepted fact that money was the key to good intelligence. It was likewise recognized as a danger. For, captured and under torture or duress, a weakening agent can be lured to the enemy cause with promises of money. It is only one more step to the maintenance of contact with both camps; and the "double agent" is born, the most treacherous, the most diabolical and venal of all personalities.

A well-known story of this kind involved the German spy who was captured in London and was used to dupe his own operators. For a period of months, under Allied control, the young German kept radio contact with his "control" in Germany, feeding German Intelligence whatever information the Allied services wished them to have. It was a successful operation from our standpoint, but a disaster for the Germans. However, they more than evened the score with the capture and control of a Dutch resistance operation being directed from London. In this case the bribe was subtle. Sensing that the young Allied spy would refuse to cooperate with them if offered money for his betrayal, the Germans held out a different kind of bait. They assured him that they would guarantee the safety of all of his contacts, provided he continued to talk with London. Should he refuse, death to them all would be the result. The spy cooperated and thereby opened up for German Intelligence a direct contact to London and cut them in on Allied resistance and sabotage operations in the area for a period of almost two years. By some appalling mischance, the Allied spy's constant warning (through a prearranged code) that he was sending under duress went unnoticed.

The smart intelligence operative will always, if possible, assimilate and use a captured spy. The variations on the theme are limitless. The motives, for the spy involved, may range from personal interest through entrapment, monetary gain, or perhaps revenge. Seldom is the defection, in war, prompted by political or ideological motives. One may work for the enemy, after capture, through fear of torture or death. One may turn double agent through unwitting entrapment so that, to save his network and his fellow agents, he must cooperate with the enemy, always hoping that his "control" back at base has been alerted to the sudden switch. One may, rarely in our own experience, turn double agent for fantastic money gain, or for the most damnable of all reasons: revenge against some other agent. But no matter what the motive or the circumstance, the double agents lives on a tightrope. Only it is a tightrope with a slow-burning fuse hitched to one end.

59

Then, in this game of madness compounded by deception, there is the rare individual who is trained, equipped, briefed, and dispatched with the express purpose of becoming an agent of the enemy. For this type of assignment one must find an individual of high intelligence and cunning, limitless nerve and daring, and blessed with a personality and magnetism capable of charming anyone within range. Such an individual was Gina.

Gina was a young Italian woman who had just passed her thirtieth birthday when the OSS first made contact with her. Tall, lean, sun-bronzed, with black hair and eyes. Gina was good-looking without being beautiful. She didn't need beauty. Gina had something more, the intangible that escapes descriptive words, something electric, dynamic, and pervasive about her that attracted followers, admirers, one could almost say slaves. She came from a middle-class background in one of the large industrial cities of Italy, and in checking her out we discovered that she had been well educated, had been fired with a political awareness that was anti-Fascist during Mussolini's regime, and was an inspired leader. It was not surprising that she should have joined up with the partisans in Italy in an all-out effort to help the Allies and overthrow the Fascist and Nazi dictatorships.

Long before we had airlifted her out of Italy for the special training required of her particular assignment. Gina had worked with an OSS-supplied-and-directed partisan unit. Her hair cut short, her naturally flat-chested figure strapped firm, she wore the clothes of a man, the rough, tattered, nondescript camouflage of the hit-and-run guerrilla fighters. Intimately familiar with the rugged mountain terrain in which her group operated, Gina proved the equal of any man in the unit. She bore her share of supplies, dragged heavy equipment along with the rest of them, did courier and lookout service, and was not averse to setting the charges necessary to the blowing up of supply dumps, rail lines, fuel depots, and the like.

Then, when the leader of her group was killed by a German sniper, Gina, the only woman in the small band of saboteurs, was the overwhelming choice of them all to become the new leader. With skill, cunning, shrewdness, and courage, Gina took over the harassment of the Germans. Nor did she miss any opportunity to embarrass and discommode the minions of the hated Mussolini. In her own little private war, in her isolated mountain sector, Gina carried on her own special brand of sabotage with marked success. But such talent could not be wasted in the slogging brutality of sabotage. Gina was tapped for a special assignment.

The first time I saw her, she was dressed in the khaki battle dress of a British commando. And except for the extra fineness of the features, the smallness of bone, and a femininity of gestures, she could have passed for a man. The black eyes returned my look with a steady, challenging sternness, the voice was full and throaty, and there was a certain swagger to the carriage of the body that could deceive the casual glance.

Several weeks later, when her training was complete, I saw the feminine side of Gina. It was just before she was to leave on her mission, and we dined together in London, quite quietly. Her hair, still short, was coiffed into a mass of curls, and there was a tiny scarlet bow of velvet tucked into it. It was the only adornment she wore. No jewellery other than a tiny gold wristwatch with a black cord band, and yet the simple, almost tailored cut of the dark blue silk dress gave her an elegance that made heads turn. Not for the beauty. It wasn't there. But for the presence, for that commanding, electric personality that sparkled of itself and made itself known wherever it went. And I can remember her absorption as we talked. Not the false, pretended interest of so many women, but the concentrated, totally engaged involvement that she projected toward me. In short, she was the fascinating woman. And as I said good night to her later that evening, I to go on with my London assignment, she, two nights later, to be dropped into northern Italy to begin an assignment of enormous complexity and danger, I felt no doubt as to the ultimate success of her mission. What I did not know was that nearly two years would go by before I was to see her again and get her story.

Italy, in her joint military operations with Germany, was the most unfortunate of allies. And it was as much from a mismating of temperaments as it was from the grating of German arrogance against Italian pomposity. The regimented, drilled, precise German mind basically held no respect for the volatile, artistic, dreaming Italian spirit. The result was that the Germans held the Italians in a kind of tolerant disregard. They were, with purpose, uninformed allies of the Nazis, never fully trusted, seldom consulted, only used. Into the midst of this Gina was dropped.

OSS had been zealous in training Gina to make the most of the German–Italian irritations. It had not been difficult When first recruited, she already had a hatred of Mussolini and all that he stood for, but it was a hatred a trifle tempered with an amused awareness of the "opera-bouffe" character of his posturings. Her attitude toward the Nazis was more intense, and it was not qualified by anything other than a fierce loathing for Nazi brutality. In her months of service with the partisans in the rugged mountain areas of Italy, she had seen the unbelievable sadism of Nazi torture techniques. So, like a religious convert, she was almost more rabidly pro-American than we could have hoped.

Gina had gone in with only the barest outline of a mission. It was the spring of 1943, long before the Allied landings on the boot of southern Italy. It was of the greatest importance for us to gather whatever information we could about German-Italian preparations against the landings they must have known would occur. Troop deployment and strength, air cover, types and concentration of planes, strategic areas like fuel depots, ammunition dumps, communications centres, information about all of this and whatever else might in any way relate to it would be of vast importance in the framing of Allied strategy. We would supply the funds necessary to her work. We would offer contacts as they might be needed, but only if needed, at her request. It would be for her to build her mission, form her plan for operation.

To recall it now, it all seems so simple. And yet it was done in the midst of the enemy, when suspicion and treachery lay at every turn, when the restrictions and privations of war made the most minor incident a potentially major problem.

Gina's family lived in the better residential area of a thriving industrial city. Her father, a second-echelon executive in a concern deeply involved with war *matériel*, was prosperous enough to maintain an attractive stone house of considerable size set in a garden of patterned flower beds, small pools, and the inevitable statuary the Italians so love to collect and display. There were two sons in the family, and they both had escaped military service by finding refuge in the plant where their father worked, in "essential" jobs. Her mother, with the quiet self-effacement of a woman of her class, presided over a collection of maids and ran the house. It was from here that Gina decided to begin her operations for us.

The family, of course, knew nothing of her service with the partisans, of her airlift to London and her training and assignment by the OSS. At the start of the war there had been many heated political discussions within the family, and they knew at the time that Gina was anti-Mussolini. Then, one day after a discussion that had shown a certain softening in her opposition to the Fascist regime, she announced that she was leaving for Rome to work in a secretarial position with a government agency. What she did not tell her family was that the "secretarial position" was as a recruiting and organizing officer. And that the "government agency" was the budding anti-Fascist organization even then beginning to build its clandestine force to fight Mussolini's dictatorship.

From this she had gone actively into the partisan groups, and by the time we had recruited her for the OSS, she was a clever, experienced, astute, and sophisticated undercover agent. Through it all, her work in Rome in 1939 and 1940, then her roving assignments and increasing partisan activity through 1941 and 1942, Gina had kept her contact with her family, had visited them for weekends, spent vacations with them, and generally deceived them into believing that she was in fact holding some sort of government position in Rome. They would have been horrified could they have seen her, dressed as a man, slogging through the snow and mud of some of Italy's roughest terrain in the harassment of both German and Italian forces. They would have been even more horrified had they known that the money she was spending, that her very maintenance was supplied by a clandestine American agency.

But when, in the spring of 1943, she suddenly reappeared at home and announced that she had left her job in Rome, that she would stay with the family for a while if that was agreeable, and that she would like to seek further employment more closely involved with the war, she was welcomed with no questions. Her mother and father were delighted to have their daughter once more with them. Her brothers were completely unconcerned. It was an ideal beginning, the perfect base for the start of her mission.

For the first two weeks Gina simply lived quietly at home and led the ordinary daily life of a young Italian girl of good family, with good connections and unattached. The war had brought many new faces to the city, mostly military, and there were not only many young Italian officers available, but there were increasing numbers of Germans assigned there for various reasons, all relating to the war.

Finding a job was no problem. It was now considered "chic" to be involved in war work, and all of the young women were frantically showing their patriotism and energy by doing war jobs. They never mentioned the fact that it also brought them into closer contact with more men than they had ever before known in their restricted Italian lives. But for Gina there was more than just a job at stake. It had to be a good one, strategically placed and with the proper potential.

Her father was the unwitting dupe in her first placement. As an executive in a firm involved in vital war work for both the Italian and German governments, he not only had many contacts with the higher ranking officers of both countries, but he also had their confidence. It was only the matter of a phone call, a short conversation, and Gina was on her way to be interviewed by a young Italian colonel for a secretarial position in a highly sensitive office. The whole episode is a perfect example of the chilling danger of trust, simple faith in personal contact without thorough checking where military security is concerned. It also demonstrates the cool assurance of the professional agent in the ability to deceive and win.

Gina was quickly cleared through the outer gates, the waiting rooms, the orderlies and secretaries because her father was known to the colonel and trusted. The way had been cleared for her by one telephone call, and by the time she had reached the outer gate the word had come down from above and she was taken directly to the colonel. He was waiting for her when she was shown into his office.

He was tall, slender, Italian-dark, and fairly good-looking, perhaps in his forties. He came to the door to meet her, his hand extended, and there was a smile on his face as he spoke. She was quick to notice that he took a sweeping physical inventory of her as she approached, and she was glad that she had worn a feminine outfit, low-cut and provocative. He motioned her to a chair as he closed the door, and he was polite almost to the point of deference. He asked after her father and mother, spoke of his admiration for her father, and kept the conversation on a social plane for some minutes. Then, in a casual, by-the-way manner, he got around to the idea that perhaps she would be interested in something useful in the war effort. It was almost as if she would be doing them a favour by going to work for them. They were desperate for people, capable people, reliable people, and there were many interesting positions available. What could she do?

Gina took over from there. She could do all types of secretarial work. She could do basic research like the scanning of intelligence reports. She watched his reaction as she mentioned intelligence and then went on to say she had had some experience with intelligence while working in Rome. She was careful not to dwell on the matter, but she was encouraged to see that the colonel, making notes as she talked, jotted this down with an underline. She could, she went on, type and take shorthand, she knew how to operate a switchboard, and she could speak and understand French, German, and English. The colonel was impressed. Also, and this brought another underlined notation on the pad, she had some familarity with cryptography. Not too much, she said, playing it in low key, but enough so that she was not completely lost in the intricacies of codes and ciphers. She made no mention of the fact that she could also handle a radio transmitter. That, she figured, would be skating a trifle too close to the veneer of her deception.

She had watched the colonel constantly as she talked. She saw his interest change to admiration, and by the time she had finished with her background, he was fascinated with the brilliance of the package that was being offered to him.

She then played her trump card.

With cool efficiency she reached into the large, shiny black handbag she was carrying and produced a sheaf of papers. These, she told the colonel, might be of value in establishing her authenticity, her ability, her work record, and her reliability. And she placed on his desk all of the necessary papers. There was her identity card. There were work cards, police passes, ration cards, all of the usual, necessary bits of paper needed in wartime Italy. But there was more. There was a pass to permit entry into the War Ministry in Rome. There was a security pass stating that she was cleared for access to any and all secret information up to the very highest classification; this pass carried the signature of the chief of Italian Intelligence. There was a three-page work record showing where she had worked, for how long and in what capacity, all in Rome and all in government positions of sensitivity and importance. And clipped to this file was a small, elegant sheet of heavy notepaper. It carried the Fascist symbol engraved at the top, it congratulated Gina ————— for outstanding work for the state "in a special capacity", and it was signed boldly by Benito Mussolini.

What the colonel did not know was that every single item lying before him on his desk had been produced and forged for Gina by OSS experts in London. And they had been part of her equipment when she was dropped into Italy at the beginning of her mission.

They had to be impressive. Gina and her advisers in London had figured that, to work, this ruse would have to be so overwhelmingly solid as to preclude any further checking or verification. The various cards and passes, even including the security pass and the congratulatory note from Il Duce, could be reasonably safe from detection. But the work record, the listing of jobs she never had, dates and places that could be checked against file records in Rome, this was a hazard. The only way to make it effective, it was reasoned, would be to have all supporting papers of such weight that further verification would look not only unnecessary, but rather ridiculous.

The colonel perused them all. He was obviously impressed with the card bearing the signature of the Chief of Intelligence giving security clearance. And he almost, as Gina related it, stood and gave the Fascist salute when he read the note with Mussolini's signature.

He rang for his secretary. And while Gina sat quite coolly across from him, he dictated a memorandum for the file stating that, on the basis of previous experience and all clearances of the highest possible category, further delay in the utilization of Gina's services would not be necessary. He stated that, as colonel in charge of the military command where she would be employed, he would take full responsibility for her immediate assignment. He further specified that a listing of all pertinent documents should be appended to the memorandum, but that the originals should be left with the young lady in question. Then, smiling at Gina, he said that she could wait in his office, that they could have a further friendly chat while his secretary made the necessary notations, and then she could take all of her papers with her.

Ten minutes later the papers were in her hands. A work form, filled out by the secretary from her other papers, was put forth for her signature, and Gina was ready to leave. The colonel was all grace and charm as he walked with her to the door. He mouthed many platitudes and banalities about the high patriotism of war work such as she would be doing, hoped that they might lunch on occasion, and told her to report to him three days hence to begin her work. He would then, he said, introduce her to her co-workers.

Three days later she began her work. It involved the scanning of field reports from the Italian Air Force involving in-action performance of planes and their armament, with special attention to weaknesses of performance, design, and the like. It meant close work with not only the Air Force, but also her father's plant and two other component factories in the area.

It was a nice beginning.

Gina lived with one haunting fear.

There was always the possibility that some avid, over-zealous underling in the personnel division would follow through on her file and check with the offices in Rome where she had said she had worked. But then, as she shrugged quite blandly after it was all over, every agent lives with fear. It is part of the picture. "It sharpens your wits," as she said, "and keeps you on your toes." And yet, as far as she herself was concerned, her situation as an agent was not ideal. She was, from necessity, operating under her own name, and she was living at home, not the most perfect of bases for clandestine work. And though she was already producing intelligence of vast importance to us, it is interesting to note that she never really considered herself fully operational until she had in fact become the double agent she had set out to be, actually operating in a secret assignment for the enemy while turning it all in to us.

Soon after she began her job with the Italian Air Force, Gina had signalled us for a contact, someone to whom she could deliver the intelligence she was gathering for transmission to us. It was impossible, under the circumstances, for her to operate a transmitter. Her life was too regimented, her time too much accounted for between home and office for her to carry on any secret contact direct with London. So we sent her a radioman, a young Italian-American trained especially for the transmission of code messages. Gina thoughtfully got him a job as a gardener at her father's house. It made her contact with him at once more easily managed and dependable. It also provided us with an almost constant stream of strategic intelligence on the condition, location, and potential of the whole air-power structure in Italy.

The Allied landings at Salerno and the subsequent withdrawal of Italy from the war gave Gina the chance she had hoped and planned for, the chance to operate full scale as a double agent. She had built her foundations well.

Sometime during the summer of 1943 Gina had moved out of her family's house. It was all done quite naturally, starting with a vacation rental of a small villa with three other girls from her office. From that she came back to a tiny flat shared with one other girl. This arrangement was a deliberate cover, and it lasted long enough for her to discover what she really wanted: a house of her own. It took a bit of time, but when she got it the set-up was ideal. On the fringes of the town, it was a small stone house set atop a hill with a view of the countryside in every direction. This meant relative safety from any surprise visits. There was a solid stone wall surrounding the property—good protection. The only road passed the gate some four hundred yards from the house—privacy. Gina "staffed" her house with an old cook borrowed from her mother and a gardener wheedled from her father. The gardener just happened to be the young Italian-American agent we had sent out to her from London to act as her radio contact. This was the solid base from which she was to operate for us for the next eighteen months.

She had made other vitally important preparations. From the very start of her work with the Italian Air Force, Gina had cultivated the colonel. It had not been difficult. He was attractive, and from his first interview with her it was obvious that he was impressed with her, not only as a fascinating young woman, but as the daughter of an executive of some importance. She had accepted his first invitation to lunch, there had been others, and then there were parties, small gatherings of the military. At these there were often young German officers, who were quickly fascinated by the dark, vital, witty young woman who spoke fluent German. It wasn't long before Gina was lunching and dining with the Germans in cosy groups. After all, their camaraderie seemed to imply, we are all involved in the same type of work, what more reasonable than to make the hours after work pleasant with people one can trust?

The Italian surrender in September 1943 produced a certain strain. Gina ignored it. The thinly disguised German disgust and contempt for the Italians made all contacts difficult, but Gina was determined not to let them interfere with her operations. And they didn't.

Early on, she had spotted the German counterintelligence man assigned to their group, and she decided to concentrate on him. He was the usual arrogant, blond, ruddy young Nazi, and his admitted job of "liaison" was so obviously phony he might as well have worn a shoulder patch worded "SPY". He had invited her to lunch with him on several occasions previous to the Italian surrender, and she was aware that his interest was purely professional, that he was anxious to find out as much about her and her job for the Italian Air Force as he possibly could. She helped him. She gave him tantalizing glimpses of what she might know, whom she might know. She dropped names. And she never let him forget that her father was by now second in command in a plant of vital importance to a certain phase of the war effort.

As she said later, he was almost too easy. He came on, step by step, blindly led to do exactly what she wanted him to do. For when, over lunch one day, she told him in heated terms that she disagreed with the Italian surrender decision, that she would do anything, *anything*, to push the Americans back into the sea, he took the bait.

Three days later, at a quiet dinner, he suggested that she might be of use to the German cause "in some special assignment".

It was a bizarre and macabre assignment, Gina's first mission for the Germans. And it gave us a glimpse into the methods employed by the Nazis in their use of espionage agents.

They were greatly concerned, the Germans, with the extent

and potential danger of the Italian disaffection after the surrender. There had been many instances of treachery, and there had been several important Italians who had refused to cooperate with the Germans in any way. After the surrender their defiance was strengthened, sure, as they were, that the Allied forces would eventually triumph and drive the Germans from Italy. It would be important to know a few key facts in the situation.

The young German counterintelligence officer explained the mission to her. There had been, he told her, a quite prominent older woman who had been dangerously anti-German. She had been warned several times over the months by the local German commanders, and she had at last been taken into custody. It was a purely restictive measure, the young Nazi quickly assured Gina, and she had not been mistreated or tortured. They had hoped that she might cooperate, perhaps even be induced to work actively for the German cause in exchange for her freedom. It was unfortunate, he continued, that she had been violently defiant and had to be disposed of. When he saw the stricken expression on Gina's face, he added hastily that it had been done humanely. She had been shot.

Now, he explained with a smile, Gina would carry on the work of the dead woman, in her name. It would be only a short assignment, and it could be quite a bit of fun, he said. After all, no one really knew yet that the woman was dead—that is, no one but a few trusted members of the German counterintelligence. But with the important name it would be of value to certain German commanders seen in her company, entertained by her, and generally accepted.

They had her full dossier. They had photographs, detailed descriptions of mannerisms, inflections, tone of voice, everything that would make the deception possible. They had a wig. Most important of all, they had the house in which she had lived in Rome. With typical German thoroughness they had taken over her house when she was arrested. They had also dismissed her servants, and they had moved in a couple of officers and a staff. It would be quite simple, they told Gina, for her to go back to the house disguised as the woman, live there for a time, and be known as entertaining the Germans. They would be careful not to expose her to any of the woman's close friends, they assured her.

Gina resigned her job with the Italian Air Force, much to

the regret of the colonel. She sent her cook back to her mother and closed the rented house where she had been living, but left the young Italian-American gardener there in a wing of the house as caretaker. Without telling anything of her plans, she arranged with him to wait there for further word from her, to alert London that she might be out of touch for two or three weeks, to be extra-cautious while she was gone, as she was certain that there would be inquiries about her absence. To her family she explained that, after all, with Italy out of the war her services were no longer needed. She was going to Venice.

The assignment, Gina said afterwards, *was* fun. She was whisked south of Rome in a German command car. The blond Nazi counterintelligence officer bade her good-bye after in-introducing her to her two companions for the trip, a man and a woman. And for the first time since her return to Italy she dropped her real name. As they had arranged, the counter-intelligence officer presented her to the two companions by a cover name. She had practised writing it in the preceding days, she had repeated it over and over, and as if to meet the OSS on its own ground, the Germans had supplied her with all necessary passes and credentials made out in the name of the dead woman. She had been careful to bury all of the documents we had supplied back at her rented villa.

They drove at night, a heavily built German enlisted man as chauffeur, the middle-aged German officer seated in front beside him. The woman, also middle-aged, coarse-looking and lean, sat in the back with Gina. She was dressed in the black uniform of a housekeeper. There was no conversation, only a guttural, sharp comment now and then between the two men. It was a relief, therefore, to Gina when the car, about half an hour out of Rome, turned off the road, passed down a short lane, and halted at a pair of huge iron gates. There was a guard post, the chauffeur showed his pass, the officer spoke a few words, and the car went on, down a long drive between rows of dark, spire-like cedars; then, suddenly circling on the gravel, they stopped before the wide stone steps of an impos-ing villa. It was completely dark except for the hooded lights of the command car, but the huge bulk of the house made itself felt like a formal cloud in the night.

The officer left the car quickly, there was a sudden brief slit of light, and he was inside the villa. Moments later the slit of light showed at the doors, then darkness, and then he was beside the car holding the door for Gina and the German woman to get out.

"Just inside. First door, right." The German officer chopped the words as the woman stepped from the car.

Motioning to Gina, the woman walked quickly up the stone steps and into the villa. The hall was large and brightly lighted, but they passed so hurriedly that Gina had only the impression of much ornate gold filigree work. Then they were in the first room on the right. It was a small salon, wood-panelled, with high ceilings, heavy damask draperies, bare parquet floors, and tapestried chairs, a sofa, a desk, a huge crystal chandelier sparklingly clean.

They waited only a few minutes and were joined by another woman. She was younger than the one accompanying Gina, and there was more refinement about her, a look of breeding, but it was coupled with a cold, clinical detachment in everything she did that was disquieting. She introduced herself and spoke directly to the German woman, saying all was ready, and then, turning to Gina, asked if she spoke German. When Gina said that she did, the words became less incisive. Everything was ordered, precise, direct.

Gina was told to strip. To the bare skin. She said that she would like to use the lavatory and was told abruptly that she might, but not just at the moment. She must strip first.

She undressed a trifle self-consciously, the two German women watching her closely. And as she pulled the last stocking from her leg, the older woman who had travelled with her took her clothes and started examining them inch by inch. Every hem, every seam, every tuck and fold of the various garments was scanned and tested, read like braille. Gina felt her blood rising at the insolence of this unexpected routine. But there was more to come.

The younger woman, now that Gina was naked, asked her to lie down on a long, bare wooden table located against one wall of the room. The wood was hard and cold, and she eased herself on to its surface. Almost as her head touched the tabletop, the young German woman approached her. She had now donned a white surgeon's smock, a stethoscope, and a headband with a strong spotlight and magnifying glass attached. Starting with her hair, she examined every inch of Gina's body. The scalp, the ears, the eyes, nostrils, lips, mouth and teeth, even deep into the throat, the tiniest hiding place was probed. For what? Gina could only wonder. Were they looking for some secret code, some telltale message, some suicide pill or instrument? Not a word was spoken to give her a clue. And the probe went on.

Under her arms, her breasts, her navel, her pubic hair. The German woman went further. Gina was subjected to a thorough and deep vaginal examination, and when that was done, there was an equally probing rectal examination. Nor did it stop there. Her legs, the backs of her knees, between her toes and under her nails, not an inch of her was left unsearched.

She had been quite unready for this treatment, and her first reaction was one of violent rebellion. Fortunately she was disciplined enough to utter not one word of complaint, not one comment of impatience. Rather she reacted as if the whole process were only routine and to be expected. From her first discussion of her mission with the young Nazi counterintelligence officer, Gina had sensed intuitively that this particular assignment was tailored to her order. Something about the whole scheme made her feel uneasy, as if the plan were not so much to gain useful intelligence for the Germans as to test her stamina and temperament as a secret agent. This fitted perfectly into that picture.

But there was one final indignity. When the examination was complete and she was told she could get down from the table, Gina again asked if she might go to the lavatory. The permission was quickly granted. But the black-uniformed travelling companion went with her, held open the door of the toilet cubicle, and observed her every gesture. It made her seethe with rage.

The older woman escorted Gina back from the lavatory to the same panelled salon. The younger German woman was still there, but she had removed her white smock, put aside her examining equipment, and was inspecting and sorting a collection of sombre clothing spread over the back of the sofa. The two German women exchanged a few curt comments as to the procedure and then, turning to Gina, the younger woman explained that she would now be dressed for her assignment in Rome. From the skin out, she would be dressed as the dead Italian woman she was to impersonate. And with a certain triumphant pride the younger woman explained that the clothing she would be wearing was not "like" that worn by the dead woman. It was her own clothing, brought from her house in Rome for the purpose. The idea made Gina's flesh crawl.

Underpants, brassière, petticoats, slip, they were all slightly démodé, from another era, with much lace and embroidered embellishment. The quality was of the finest, and everything was laundered and ironed to perfection, denoting the background of the woman to whom they had belonged, the woman Gina was now preparing to impersonate. The dress was of a heavy black silk, with long sleeves and a high neckline, relieved with only a suggestion of delicate white lace. And there were black silk stockings and softly burnished, hand-made black kid pumps. They were a trifle small for Gina, and they pinched when she first walked in them, but the soft suppleness of the leather made them bearable. There was not the slightest suggestion on the part of either of the German women that perhaps she might be more comfortable in her own shoes.

When she had dressed, a wig was produced from a large box. The hair was long, it was iron-grey with a few rather elegant streaks of white, and it was coiffed into a high-piled soft arrangement. Just a touch old-fashioned, and yet with a kind of ageless chic. There was a jewelled pin clipped into it high at the back, and Gina noted with the eye of a sophisticate that the jewels were real.

The younger German woman asked her to sit on a low stool and then deftly bound her short-cropped hair with a length of bandage-like material. She fastened it securely, and when it was in place to her satisfaction, she slipped the wig on to Gina's head. It was all done with cold precision, and Gina remarked to herself that neither of the German women showed any of the usual feminine excitement and flurry that would normally accompany the dressing and arranging of one's hair or costume. There was no light banter, no quick exclamation of pleasure or surprise. Rather, they worked with the quiet intensity of a couple of mechanics on a motor.

Clothes on, the wig in place, a large make-up box was produced. And alongside was a series of small, clear-cut glossy photographs of a rather distinguished-looking older woman. No effort was made to show Gina the face she was to carry, but from the sideways glimpses she could get of the photos,

74

she recognized a certain basic resemblance between herself and the older face—the forehead and chin lines, the straight nose. Full-face, full-face from an elevated angle and from below, right and left profiles, three-quarters, the Germans had done their photographic planning with thoroughness. And it occurred to Gina with a chilling suddenness that the intelligence operatives who had taken the old woman into custody mut have had this very deception in mind while she was still living. They must have decided well in advance to kill her and then to impersonate her for their own sadistic purposes. It must have taken an unusually cruel and brutal mentality that could so thoroughly "blueprint" the physical features of an old woman with the express purpose of putting her to death and planning her impersonation.

The whole nightmare of the dead woman haunted her. What had she done? Why should she have been of such importance to the Germans? Where was her family? Who were her contacts? Why had they killed her? These and dozens of related questions churned within her mind as the two German women worked over Gina's face. They were questions that would never be answered.

There was one last detail before they had completed the physical transformation of Gina into an older Italian woman of obviously aristocratic background. There was the slight matter of the teeth. The younger German woman, whom the other one had begun calling "Doctor", explained that she would now work on the mouth if Gina would "open, please." From her file she produced a set of gruesome, revolting photographs of the old woman's teeth. They were close-ups, and from the visible clamps holding back the lips, the lifeless pallor of the face, and the glazed look of the eyes, they had obviously been done after death. What they showed was that the old woman was missing one lower-front tooth, slightly left of centre, and that there was a gold crown on an upper side tooth and a bit of gold bridgework.

The "Doctor" produced complete replicas of the goldwork from a small box. It was soft and easily malleable, and with a few deft pressures she set them in place over Gina's perfectly sound teeth. A similarly pliant casing of black plastic was slipped into place to indicate the gap in the old woman's lower jaw. At least they had not pursued realism to the extent of extracting one of Gina's perfectly good teeth. She had half expected it, and she was relieved that there were limits beyond which she would not have to go for her mission.

They were now exchanging short grunts of comment, the two German women, looking first at Gina and then at their photographs of the old woman. They circled her, squinting and studying, and at last they told her she could stand and look at herself, her new self. Gina walked to a tall mirror against one wall, and as she approached her own reflection, she was startled by the transformation. Her hair, her face, her figure, they were completely, convincingly, of someone else, someone she had never known, would never know. The "Doctor" handed her a full-length photograph of the dead woman dressed in the very clothes Gina was then wearing. The effect was astonishing. The hair, the lines of the face, the tiny crinkles about the eyes, the sparse eyebrows, the grey sag of the cheeks, they were there in the photograph and they were there on her. She felt a sudden grudging admiration for her creators.

There was one final touch. From a rose-red box such as would come from Cartier's, white-satin-lined, the "Doctor" produced a large clip and pinned it to the right shoulder of the black dress, just where it was placed in the photograph. It was an important clip, and it was of diamonds, emeralds, and sapphires.

The "Doctor" left the room, but not before she had cleared away the various cosmetics she had been using. She was gone a few minutes, leaving Gina with the older German woman. Then suddenly there were voices, and she was back with an officer ramrod-straight, balding, in an immaculate uniform and highly polished boots. He came toward Gina, spoke in good, if German-accented, Italian and complimented her on her appearance. He looked long at the photographs, then at Gina, and again at the photographs, turning, studying, searching for the flaw. There was a long, strained silence during which Gina felt uncomfortably like some damaged commodity about to be rejected by a potential buyer. Then, in quick, curt tones he complimented the two German women, and almost as an afterthought, introduced himself to Gina. He was a major, and he announced that he would brief her on the specifics of her mission.

He would go into Rome with her and would be one of the "guests" in "her" house. She would also be accompanied by the older German woman, who was set up to play the role of her housekeeper. Gina was not pleased with this news. She had taken a dislike to the coarse, stolid, rather sinister woman whose whole demeanour was one of condescension and suspicion. From the first she had felt under surveillance in her presence and she had not liked the search of her clothing or the intimate supervision of her use of the lavatory. But now, with the subterfuge of the housekeeper, Gina was convinced that the woman's sole purpose was to check on her every move, her every contact, her every gesture. It was a disquieting situation.

The major gave her other instructions. It was all quite simple, he explained, really. Only to go and live in a large house in Rome where everything would be taken care of and she, Gina, would play the part of the chatelaine. There were to be one or two receptions for the German hierarchy in Rome. There would be some top Italian officials present. She would be there, in the background, lending "her" presence and "her" house for its propaganda value. He placed a special emphasis on the "her" aspect of the situation. He watched her intently as he spoke. It might seem, on the surface, like a lot of trouble to go to for a staged propaganda effect, he emphasized, but there were reasons, deeper reasons, for the ruse. Perhaps some day she would understand.

Gina was sure she understood already. She was now convinced that this was a controlled testing of her ability as an agent. Just possibly the old woman might have been of enough importance to have had a certain influence in Rome, but she still found it difficult to believe that such an elaborate deception could be justified by such purely ephemeral effects as "public" reaction. It was, she was certain, a "laboratory" testing of an agent, the "laboratory" being one private house in Rome, the agent being herself. At least this was the conviction with which she pursued her mission.

It was late morning when they left the villa and headed for Rome. And now the pattern had changed. Gone was the German staff car in drab military paint with the enlisted man as driver and the officer beside him. Instead there was a black sedan, there was a young Italian in chauffeur's livery at the wheel, and the "housekeeper", the surly German woman whom Gina distrusted, sat in the front seat beside him. On the back seat with Gina sat the German major.

One thing especially fascinated Gina about this short trip

77

of perhaps half an hour. They were in war, there was war activity everywhere, troops, equipment, *matériel*, and if that were not enough, there were all of the tensions and strains, the suspicions and controls of a compact recently broken, the Italian surrender. In ordinary circumstances it would have made any kind of travel difficult, if not impossible. But not for them. They drove fast. They were unimpeded. And when they came to the inevitable checkpoints and roadblocks, there was only a slowing of speed—no passes to show, no inspections, no probes, no delays. She watched every move of the young chauffeur, of the German "housekeeper", for some signal some code gesture of clearance. There was nothing she could discover. Yet something, some mark perhaps on the front of the car, some small symbol, cleared their way like magic. It was unthinkable that German efficiency could have alerted every command post for clearance, and besides that would open a seam in the security wrapping of a clandestine mission. It absorbed her attention for the silent journey.

They were well into Rome when the major beside her spoke quietly in German. There would be no need for hurry as she left the car, she should walk slowly into the house, she would be "home" soon. There was no other conversation.

Then there were high, solid stone walls, there were enormous solid double doors from the street. Gina remarked that they opened silently, well oiled by German efficiency. Under Italian control, she was sure, they would have jerked, squealed, and creaked. They were in a courtyard, fully enclosed, and came to a stop before an imposing entrance with high grilled doors. She was "home".

It was a small palazzo. There was much marble, elegant carved panelling, mirrors, paintings, and crystal. There was, she discovered that afternoon as she inspected the house with her "housekeeper", much fine furniture and great taste displayed. There were small salons, a dark-panelled library with painted beams across the high ceiling, a large dining-room, and an even larger reception room with polished floor, mirrored walls, and a magnificently painted ceiling. This, she was told, was where the receptions would be held. They were all, for Gina, haunted by the spectre of the woman she was impersonating.

Three days later the German command held the first reception. It was quite a show. Work details had spent several days scrubbing and polishing the old house until everything glistened and sparkled under the lights as it must have done only when it was new. The huge doors at the street were bathed in soft light, and they were flanked by guards in dress uniform, brass polished, leather buffed, clothing creased. More guards ringed the inner courtyard, flanked the grilled doors, and lined the steps into the marble entrance hall. A young, handsome, very Nordic Nazi captain stood at the top of the stairs to check the guest list and direct the guests to the large reception room. There a major, the very major who had accompanied Gina from the villa where she had been briefed, met and escorted the guests to the reception line. And there, flanked by a colonel and a general, stood Gina. There were flowers, there was music, and there was champagne, the best the Germans could get out of France for the occasion.

The guest list was a mixed bag. Every German officer of importance in Rome was there. There was Italian officialdom, those who had escaped imprisonment or worse after the fall of Mussolini and the surrender of Italy. And there was a smattering from an old Italian woman's world, aristocrats, socialites, adventurers, most of them too weakened by war to resist the chance for free food and champagne. It occurred to Gina that perhaps not a dozen of them had ever before seen the inside of this beautiful house over which she falsely presided, and she was sure, from what she could gather of the woman she was impersonating, none of their names would ever have appeared on her guest list.

The Germans had organized it well. Not for one moment was Gina left alone with a guest. As soon as the formal receiving was broken up and the party became general, Gina was constantly escorted by at least two German officers. They monopolized her time, they kept her moving, seen, present but never available to any of the Italian guests for more than a passing word, a nod, a smile. And when at last the party broke up toward midnight, Gina, strained and nervously exhausted, felt as old as she looked.

There was a second shift. Soon after the last of the formal guests had left and Gina had gone to her room with the German "housekeeper" in attendance, a second party took place. The outside lights were extinguished, the house was shuttered, and the call girls arrived. The Germans danced and drank and sexed away the night.

79

Gina stayed in the house in Rome for a trifle over two weeks. Each morning the "Doctor" arrived after breakfast to re-do her make-up, creating again each day the old Italian woman she was supposed to be. Then, before each reception, there were make-up sessions again and careful dressing in something appropriate from the large collection of clothing still hanging in the dead woman's wardrobes. It was like getting ready for the stage, making up for a play—only the play was to go on all day long and into the evening.

The Germans gave three more receptions for different groups, sending out their invitations in the name of the unfortunate Italian woman whom they had long since shot, using Gina as a kind of living "set piece", a hostess and sponsor.

It was, as she said, fun—and hell. There was the play-like character of the mission that made it fun. There was comfort, elegant surroundings, good food, excellent service, and entertainment. But there was the hell of the nightmare, of the lie. It was compounded by the hell of the German woman who never left her side except during the formal parties. And then her place was taken by an equally possessive officer, until she thought she would go out of her mind for lack of privacy.

Pervading it all and nurtured by the constant surveillance was the erosion of suspicion. Gina was convinced, and she most certainly was correct, that the whole episode was staged as a testing of her. The sudden indignity of the personal examination and search indicated distrust over and beyond the regular demands of caution in dealing with an agent. And though there might have been some vague propaganda value to the masquerade and the receptions, it was much more logical to explain the whole mission as a testing of her as an agent. Certainly the Germans were well aware of the tensions they were subjecting her to, the lack of privacy, the full-time impersonation, the fact that she knew only as much of the picture as they wished to give her. They were going further than that, they were demanding that she adapt herself to a complete disguise with all of the attendant anxieties, stresses, and challenges such deception demands.

Then suddenly it was over. The morning after the final reception, the German major appeared to escort her back to the villa where she had first been prepared for this particular mission. Still dressed as the old Italian woman, Gina descended the steps of the palazzo, stepped into the black sedan, and with the major seated beside her, was driven out of the city. There was one tremendous and pleasant change. The German "housekeeper" was not with them.

Again the quick, unimpeded trip between Rome and the villa. Again silence. Only the whirling, dust-veiled stutter of trees, houses, vehicles, the grotesquely slow-motion palsy of people. The high-speed whine, the occasional sudden, stomach-sinking lurch of instant braking, only this. No words, no glance or motion, no shared nod or shrug, no awareness of contact with the world or anyone in it, especially with the two other people sharing the car with her.

Then, to her overwhelming grateful relief, they slowed, turned from the main road, drove a short distance, and were at the gates of the villa. Only once before in her life, and then only briefly and at night, had Gina been here, and yet the gates seemed to loom with a welcoming friendliness. Such was her relief. Again the guards, the passes, and they were sent the length of the drive to come to a stop in front of the villa. It was large, palladian, and warmly yellow, with a terrace across the entire front, wide steps flanked by huge stone urns, an elegant pair of doors.

An hour later, inside, divested of her make-up and the Italian woman's clothes, dressed again in her own things, Gina found herself at lunch with the young Nazi counter-intelligence officer who had first started her on this madness. He was courteous, highly respectful, and most complimentary of her mission for them in Rome. As a token of his esteem— he used the word "our"—he gave Gina the Italian woman's clip of diamonds, emeralds, and sapphires.

Gina stayed on at the villa outside Rome for three days. They were not idle ones. Under the supervision of the Nazi counterintelligence officer, she was given a course of basic instruction in German espionage techniques. She was taught the use of invisible links, a device in which the Germans had an innocent faith. She was taught code work and ciphers. She was taught how to lie under interrogation, how to resist torture tactics of the most horrifying intensity, and how to secrete vital information in her clothing or on her body. All of this later came back to us for important usage.

And she was registered. Under a cover name, Gina was weighed, measured, photographed and fingerprinted for the

F

Nazi intelligence files. She was also numbered. Using an electric stylus, the Germans tattooed a four-digit cipher of letters and numbers into Gina's left heel. With infinitely more pain, the same four-digit cipher was tattooed into the lower, fleshy, inner surface of her right buttock not far from the rectum.

Still she had had no definite assignment for a further mission for the Germans. Her conversation with the young Nazi counterintelligence officer had remained for the most part general. It was agreed that she would work for him, that her command of English would be of tremendous value now that the Americans had landed in Italy, but the how of the work, the work itself was still to be planned. It was vital that she make contact once again with the young Italian-American radioman still waiting back at her rented house.

She handled it cleverly. It would be necessary, Gina explained to the Nazi, that she return for a few days to the north in order to close out the lease on the small house she had taken. He was reluctant to let her go, and said that the expense of the house could easily be borne by German Intelligence. Gina pointed out the folly of the expense and further stated that she should close out the lease in order to stop speculation in the neighbourhood as to her whereabouts. For a frightening moment the Nazi suggested that he would return with her, he could drive her there himself, but when she pointed out that she was known in the area, that her real identity would kill any further usefulness for German counterintelligence if she were seen with him, he relented. It was agreed that she should return alone to the north by ordinary means available to the general public. She could be back at the villa near Rome in a few days.

She made the trip quite easily. She knew that she was being tailed by a German agent. She expected it, even before she moved, and she spotted him moving along the platform in the crowded station in Rome. She saw him twice on the train, looking disinterested, preoccupied but aware. And soon after she had reached her family's house she had seen him pass by on the opposite side of the street. Her every move, she knew, would be reported back to the young Nazi waiting for her at the villa outside Rome.

For this reason alone, she delayed going out to her rented villa on the edge of town. The whole first day she did small errands about town and she made one trip to the office of the rental agent from whom she had taken the villa. Her shadow saw it all. The second day she went out to the villa. Franco, the young radio operative whom we had sent out from London for her, was there, acting his part. He was pruning some shrubbery when she arrived, and she called to him from the gate, which he had kept locked.

He let her in, and as they walked the length of the long drive to the house, she was grateful for the foresight that had made her choose a villa back from the highway. It would at least keep her shadow far enough away to make identification of Franco impossible.

Quickly and coolly, she told Franco that they were being watched. She then, in bare outline, told him that she was about to begin her real function as a double agent, that she was being given an assignment for German counterintelligence. She told him that he would have to move closer to Rome, and she told him about the villa where the Germans had set up an espionage and sabotage base, the villa where she was staying. She asked Franco to contact London, check her in as OK and operational, and ask London for a contact in the Rome area and one near Naples, where she was sure she would be asked to operate for the Germans.

They walked the garden as she talked, and she stayed only a short time. She went into the house, purely for the benefit of the agent spying on her from somewhere down the road, did a quick tour of the rooms, where she had left not one personal item, and emerged again to full view. She told Franco where she had buried her OSS-forged credentials and told him to leave them there until she might need them further. She did one last thing. She gave him, orally, repeated over and over again and later to be jotted down in some safe place by him, the tattooed code numbers on her heel and buttocks. This little detail was later to save her life.

She cautioned him against doing any transmitting for a day or two, as she was certain that the Germans would watch the house even after she had left and returned to the villa near Rome. It was imperative that they discover nothing suspicious about her. One more important detail had to be arranged: how she and Franco could keep contact. Gina was certain that, once operating for the Germans on a definite clandestine assignment, she would have freedom of movement. On this basis she agreed to meet Franco at a certain rendezvous in

Rome on the third, thirteenth, twenty-third, or thirtieth of each month, whichever date could be managed. In short, if she could not make the rendezvous on the third, he was to be there on the thirteenth; if she couldn't make the thirteenth, he should wait for her on the twenty-third, and so on until they had made contact.

Four days later, all plans made, Gina was back at the villa near Rome for more intensive training. It was then the young Nazi counterintelligence officer explained the specifics of her mission. Apparently the report from the person who had shadowed her had been in her favour, for there was slightly less tension visible in the manner of the young Nazi. It pleased her to know that her caution had paid dividends. At least she was now being accepted as a full-scale espionage operative by the Nazis.

With her knowledge of English, the young Nazi explained, it would be of value to them if she could infiltrate the Allied forces in the Naples area. She was not to speak any English. Rather, he insisted, it would be more productive for her to pretend complete ignorance of the language, but to listen, listen, listen, he kept repeating, for any and all bits of information she might pick up that would aid the German counter-offensive against the Allied troops. The Americans were un-sophisticated, friendly, and naïve, he explained, so she should have no real trouble making close contact. He gave her a knowing look as he spoke and then added, when she gave no sign of understanding his meaning, that she was an attractive woman, which was always an advantage. He was sure she would know what to do.

The landings at Salerno had taken a serious toll, he told her, and the intelligence they had been able to gather was that the Americans were seriously under-equipped, they had few reinforcements, and their morale was low. It would be well to have confirmation of all this, with specific details as to just where the weaknesses were most apparent, what they could best exploit for the Nazi cause.

For her personal "cover" the Germans had worked out an ingenious story to account for her lack of intimate knowledge of the Naples area. She would pose as a war widow. The Americans were always soft on the unfortunates in war, the young Nazi said with a sneer. That was why there was no question of an ultimate Nazi victory, they had the hardness, the ruthlessness to attain victory. The Allies were soft. But, he went on, it was a feature that could be utilized to the German advantage. Gina would pose as a young war widow who had lost not only her husband but two small children as well. She was, so the story went, originally from Rome, but she had found work in the south, an area she knew little about, and now she was caught up in the turmoil of the Allied landings and the Italian surrender, a war casualty of the periphery.

The Nazi counterintelligence officer furnished her with all of the necessary documentation for her story. There was a much worn photograph of the "dead husband", a rugged, dark Italian of about Gina's age. There were three snapshots of the children, two singles and one of the two together. They were dark, smiling, slightly sad and wistful-looking children of pre-school age. And once again she found herself haunted by a deceitful association with people she had never known or ever seen, suddenly intimately concerned with them, their lives and backgrounds. There was no effort made to explain who these people were, whether they were alive or dead, and Gina felt it best not to ask. They were like so many stage props, accessories to the part she was readying herself to play.

Of course there were all of the usual identity cards, the ration cards, the work cards, the innumerable bits of paper demanded of war controls. She was given clothes, worn, mended, tattered, and soiled to lend authenticity to her story. She was given money, plenty of it, some in lira, and a large sum in dollars, which she was cautioned to hide in a safe place as soon as she was able to establish a working base. She was cautioned, even as we cautioned our agents, to be careful of her money, never to have with her more than her circumstances would merit. The dollars, she was told, were to be used for bribes or for the purchase of important information. Lastly, she was given a couple of safe addresses and a contact in Naples. The safe addresses were to be used only if she needed to hide out. The contact, once established, would channel her intelligence findings back to the Nazi counterintelligence in Rome.

And now she was ready. With all factors double-checked in the precise German manner, Gina was turned over to a courier escort who piloted her through the German lines on the outskirts of Naples. From there she was on her own.

Everything seemed to be on the move, and everything seemed to be coming toward her. People, people, people, they were old and young, worn, weary, tattered, starving, frightened. One thing alone they had in common, the insane idea that safety lay in flight, that the city should be fled. It was the very epitome of the aimlessness, the madness of war. Old men dragging small carts loaded with the most incongruous possessions. Old women shuffling bent, broken, and rusted prams laden with false treasures, clinging to the only "things" in which they had faith. Younger women, aged to dried skeletons in mid-life, carrying, pulling, herding dirty, emaciated children too weak, too insensate to cry. All this, an endless wail of drifting humanity living and dying, defecating and urinating, never eating, only scavenging against a surrealist backdrop of dust, destruction, and noise. Whole army trains of equipment stalled along a road, Italian and German, the burned-out tank, the charred body, no more remarked than the next rock or pebble or the large piles of rubbled buildings. And in the distance the dull thud and whomp of bombs and heavy guns, the scream and whine of planes. It was all there, endlessly, over and over, there to be endured while the displaced hordes moved on, away, anywhere, somewhere, but away from where they were.

Gina made her way against the tide, and at last she was in Naples. No one, anywhere, had challenged her, no one had asked to see her work cards, her identity cards, there was a complete breakdown of control. It suited her.

"One does horrible things in war. Without thinking," I remember her saying. And then she went on to describe her first few days in Naples. How she simply wandered the streets wondering where to go, and then, quite suddenly and naturally, moved into a small abandoned house as if it were her own. How she had seen a young Italian cut down by a sniper's bullet one afternoon. And how, after dark, she had gone back to where he lay, stripped him of his clothes, all of his cards and passes, and used them for herself.

Gina had spun an incredible web of deceit for herself up to this point, and yet she was only just beginning to operate. With the careful deliberation, foresight, and daring of a skilled agent, she worked out her plans. At last, in Naples as long as she had not checked in with the contact she had been given by the young Nazi counterintelligence officer back in Rome, she had complete freedom from surveillance. She was now on her own; the haunting shadow of being tailed by the Germans no longer loomed so large, and she began to lay her plans.

First, and most important, was to make contact again with Franco. Deliberately, while still in the Rome area, she had made no effort to meet with him. She was certain that any move she might make while still at the training villa outside Rome would have been spied upon by the Germans. It would be safer, even though infinitely more time-consuming and harrowing, to wait until she was established in Naples, then to return to Rome, if only for a day. This had several advantages. First, it would practically ensure the safety of her meeting with Franco. Secondly, she would be able to give him more definite information about her operations in Naples.

She let another date go by before she made her move to contact Franco. Then, dressed in the clothes she had taken from the dead young Italian and using his papers, she made her way back to Rome. It was not, she said with a disarming simplicity, a difficult trip, even though she had to use both bus and train.

She arrived a day ahead of the rendezvous date. Rome seemed to be completely taken over by the German army, and for the first time she felt a sudden surge of fear, an uneasiness brought about by the combination of her mission, her disguise, the German control of Rome, and the fact that she had no place to stay in Rome. She decided against trying to get into a cheap hotel or a rooming house or *pensione*. It meant the scanning of too many cards, the registration with the police and all that. Mussolini's huge new rail terminal offered the best haven. And yet even that wasn't safe. The police, prodded by the Germans, campaigned constantly against vagrants and the growing horde of displaced persons coming into the city from the south. It would be impossible to curl up on a bench in the vast building anywhere after midnight.

Gina had a brilliant, if uncomfortable, solution. She spent the night seated on a toilet in a cubicle of the men's washroom in the station. It gave her the idea for later passing information to Franco.

It was mid-morning when she went to the appointed meeting place, although she had left her sanctuary in the man's room before six. Franco was waiting for her. He was seated on a bench reading a newspaper, and he paid no attention to her when she sat down at the other end of the same seat. After all, he was not expecting to see her dressed as a man. She sat for a moment watching the people passing before them and then, when she thought the time was right, she spoke the code sentence they had agreed upon. She said the words distinctly, casually, and she saw his fingers tense against the newspaper he was holding. No other sign, nothing to indicate that he had heard. She spoke the words again, and he gave the coded reply and dropped his paper. This was her cue. Gina was afraid that her disguise might take him off guard, so for the sake of any passers by who might have noticed, she quickly, with feigned surprise, rose and shook his hand as one might do to any friend suddenly discovered by chance behind the morning paper.

Franco's surprise was not feigned. He could hardly believe that the young man seated beside him was actually the young Gina he had last seen in the garden of the rented villa in the north. He clung to her hand, exclaiming over and over again his delight at seeing her. Gina couldn't help musing that, to anyone even as strongly suspicious as a lurking counter-intelligence agent, the meeting could not have seemed more genuinely unplanned, more innocent.

The sun was warming, and they sat for twenty minutes, perhaps longer, just talking and quite consciously enjoying a freedom neither of them had known since arriving in Italy on their respective missions. Gina told him how she had spent the night, perhaps the only woman in Rome ever to have spent the night in a public men's room, and they both laughed about it. There was much of importance to talk about, and there was a volume of information, technical and detailed, concerning techniques Gina had learned under the Nazi espionage tutelage that they thought should be sent on to London.

They arranged to meet again in mid-afternoon in the men's room of the station. She would be there about three forty-five, she would choose the next to the last cubicle furthest from the entrance so that, when he came in, Franco would have a choice of either the one to the right or the one to the left of hers. She would be wearing a small paper clip on each shoe fastened at the base of the laces for identification. Franco would have a small inkblot on the toe of each boot.

Gina rose from the bench, shook Franco by the hand, and said she hoped to see him again before too long. Then, turning abruptly, she swaggered away, leaving him alone again with his paper. She went to a tiny restaurant and had lunch, and then, during the midday lull that hit Rome even in the midst of war, she withdrew to a secluded corner of the Borghese gardens and, using a magazine as a cover and a table, she wrote out the vital notes for Franco to transmit to London. They were precisely done on small slips of thin tissue and they had meaning only for him to whom she had explained the background earlier in the day.

At 3.45 Gina strode into the men's room of the station again. She admitted that it took a bit more courage during the daylight hours. There were many more men in the room, washing their hands, using the urinals. She went quickly past them all, walked the line of toilet cubicles, and stopped before the next to the last. To her intense relief it was free, and she noted that the adjoining booths to either side were also unoccupied. She worked the pay catch quickly and was inside, tensed, alert, waiting. She sat on the seat and drew out her notes, scanned them to make sure they were in the proper order, and waited.

Suddenly there were footsteps. They came on, nearer, paused, went past her cubicle and stopped. She could hear the fumbled working of the catch, the closing of the door, the rustle of clothing, then quiet. A foot became just visible to her under the partition, a heavy workman's boot, mud-caked and scuffed. And there, on the toe and slightly off centre, was a dark splash of ink.

Gina slid her foot to the side, spreading her legs until her own shoes with the tiny paper clips at the laces could be seen in the next booth. Franco cleared his throat, scratched lightly on the partition, and waited. Gina rustled some paper, and in a moment she saw the tips of his fingers barely visible under the partition, far to the back, just opposite the fixture. In a split second she had the small clutch of tissue notes in his hands, and he acknowledged them with another husky clearing his throat.

Gina pulled the chain in her cubicle. There was a wonderfully loud and consoling rush of water, and before it had subsided she had unlocked the door of her cubicle and sauntered the length of the room. Past the urinals, past the washbowls, she looked neither to left nor right until she had left the station and found the freedom and the freshness of the open air.

Behind her, safe in Franco's custody, she had left some telling information. It included, along with much fascinating data on Nazi intelligence, the German safe addresses which had been given to her for use in Naples, the identity of her German contact there, and the manner in which she was to meet with him. And she had carried away with her, from her earlier talk with Franco, the identity of her OSS contact in the Naples area and the manner in which she was to make herself known to him.

An hour lated she was on her way back to Naples.

A more explosive, intricate, and dangerous espionage assignment than Gina's would be difficult to imagine. It would be almost impossible to bring off successfully without the rare combination of skill, caution, intelligence, charm, and sheer daring that made up her personality.

Here was a young woman already a veteran operative in the former employment of the Italian services. Here she was a trusted agent of the OSS, trained in our schools, equipped, financed, and dropped by us into Italy for the purpose of reporting any and all information of value to be used against the Italians and the Germans in every way possible. We had supplied her with a radio contact. We had given her a field contact in the Naples area, and she had our complete confidence. But at the same time the German counterintelligence service had recruited her, trained her, used her with confidence. And they had equipped her, financed her, given her safe addresses and a field contact in the same Naples area.

It was for her to keep the lines from crossing. It was for her to watch every move, every contact, lest somewhere the lines might cross and she would be short-circuited out of existence. Any espionage assignment is a game for keeps, a battle of wits based on deception on the one hand and credibility on the other. But the role of the double agent follows a pattern so harrowing in intensity, so terrifying in complexity, there are few who can stand the strain, who can deliver the goods, or who live to tell the story. Gina was one of the few.

The Office of Strategic Services had dropped many clandestine agents into Italy preparatory to the landings at Salerno. They had established themselves with the partisan groups, they had worked as independent teams of saboteurs, and there were those acting individually as intelligence agents. And then, soon after the landings, there had been the established OSS bases at Caserta and Bari with other hidden nests for the protection, supply, and direction of our agent chains. The personnel for these installations, for the most part, had moved up from North Africa along with or in advance of the Allied armies. From Casablanca, from Algiers, from Tunis, Oran, Alexandria, and Cairo, the concentration was now on southern Italy.

Gina had preceded them all. And she was trained, equipped, and directed from London, one of the few OSS operatives so handled, in the Italian peninsula.

She timed her operations carefully. On her return from Rome and her meeting with Franco, she made her first contact with her OSS cut-out in the Naples area. She had not yet checked in with her German contact for obvious reasons. Until she had made connection with the OSS channels in the area, Gina did not want to have any German contact. As yet her identity was unknown, her whereabouts unknown to the German service, which meant that she would be reasonably secure from surveillance through tailing. Once she had made contact with the German cut-out, her every move toward the OSS would be fraught with the most intense danger. The Germans had shown themselves to be suspicious of their agents, untrusting and cautious.

Still dressed as a man, Gina made her first contact with the OSS cut-out for her mission. Together they worked out the safest method of operation. It involved the continued disguise of herself as a man for each contact to be made with the OSS. For the rest of the time, while operating ostensibly as a German agent, and for any and all contact with the German cut-out, she would use the original cover given her by the Nazi counterintelligence officer in Rome, the pose of being a displaced young war widow.

It was perhaps ten days after her original departure from Rome on her mission for the German service that Gina made her first contact with the German cut-out in the Naples area. To her surprise he turned out to be an Italian. She had expected a German, almost without thinking about it, and yet an Italian, under the circumstances, was certainly the most obvious, the most secure choice. He was dressed in the shabby gentility of a minor office worker, but there was a rigidity of manner and bearing that pointed to a military background. One never indulged in small talk with a cut-out, no personal exchanges, so there was no way for her to pry, to discover whether or not this man had been recently of the Italian army or air force. It really didn't matter. What was more important was the fact that he was perhaps in his forties, there was a sinister coldness about him that made her uncomfortable in his presence, and he had a way of looking at her while he talked. As she said, it made her feel as if she were naked in front of him.

Before making her contact with the German cut-out, the Italian, Gina, had made other living arrangements. She had kept the abandoned house as a refuge where she could keep her male clothing, the necessary papers to go with the disguise, and all that. But to operate with the Germans she needed something away from that particular set-up. She found a single room in a small *pensione*, and she was glad that she had done it on her own. For the sinister Italian, on their first meeting, suggested that he could find her a place to live that would offer her good protection. It was a safe guess that it would also have offered her complete coverage for every moment of her life, surveillance of every move, every contact.

He was a hard taskmaster, the Italian. At that first meeting he gave Gina a listing of the things the German service wished to find out. Mostly they were routine. It was hoped, he told her, that she could get behind the Allied lines, that she could ingratiate herself with some of the Americans, gain their confidence and learn some future plans, critical troop-deployment factors, and the like. She might even admit to being able to speak English, in the hope that she could get a job an as interpreter or translator. Anything would help.

So began her work as a double agent.

Once, sometimes twice, a week Gina disguised herself as a man and met with her OSS contact. She provided him with everything she could gather from her work as a German agent. He, in turn, provided her with plenty of material to keep the Germans happy. Authentic information, something they could check out and verify, this was provided, often just too late to be of any help, but valuable enough to enhance Gina's prestige with the Germans. And then, once they had been seduced into accepting everything she gave them, the OSS fed them occasional false bits on the projected plan of some attack, a bombing raid, a major troop alignment, or the like. It all helped to add to the confusion for the Germans. They, in their turn and unwittingly, through the specifics of their requests to her for information, tipped their hand to us as to their critical weaknesses, their plans for meeting our projected assaults, their whole programme for fighting up the Italian peninsula. It was most rewarding.

This fascinating, delicate, and explosive game continued for several months.

Then it happened.

It was mid-winter Naples, cold, raw, damp as only sunny Italy can be in the depths of winter. At three, perhaps three-thirty in the morning, the war-torn city was black, stark, menacingly quiet as Gina made her way stealthily back to the abandoned house where she would change into her widow's clothing. She had just finished a most productive session with her OSS contact and had been complimented for the quality as well as the quantity of the intelligence she was providing the Allied services. If an operating agent can ever be light-hearted on a mission, then Gina was lighthearted. But it was a relative thing. She was pleased with the success of her mission and she had long since become accustomed to the demands of the double deceit she was living, but she was still sophisticated enough to be guarded in her moves, alert to any potential danger.

It was in a tattered, waterfront area of the city, her abandoned house, and she always hated the lonely, dark streets. She had learned to hunch her shoulders and move with a rolling walk in an effort to increase her stature and add to the illusion of toughness she hoped to create. But she confessed later that it was always then, on the late, deserted streets of Naples that she felt the first quakings of feminine fear. All else was nothing.

Rats scurried before her, scavenging in the dirt, rot, and rubble of the city. There was no other sign of life. Darkened warehouses, shuttered, partially wrecked shops, a bombed area, a few more crumbling buildings that may have been stores or offices or tenements, then she was there. The broken windows, the sagging door that only closed halfway, the stone steps and walls, chipped and cracked, she recognized them only as something familiar, a kind of haven. Instinctively as she approached she scanned the area for any sign of a lurking figure, ready to go on past should there be anyone around to observe her entry.

There was no one, and she slid quickly and quietly through the half-opened door. She waited just inside the door, listening, as she always did. There was no sound and she moved along the narrow hall toward a small room at the back where she had hidden her things, where she changed her clothes. It was black dark in the house and she moved slowly, groping her way, feeling the wall as she went, working toward the doorway to the room. Her hand touched the casing, she felt the door, pressed against it, and entered the small room.

In one sickening moment she was blinded by the sudden stiletto beam of a spotlight. And almost before she could move, before she could make a sound, someone had pinioned her arms from the rear. Roughly her wrists were bound behind her back with short heavy cord and then, deftly, almost in one gesture, her ankles were bound tightly together and she was prostrate on the cold stone floor of the room. She started to scream, but the sound was muffled brusquely as a gag was stuffed into her mouth and secured in place with tape.

Then the voice. It was the cold, sneering, sinister voice of the Italian who was assigned as her contact in the German service. He told her that she had nothing to fear, that she was among friends, and then he introduced her to three other men, one Italian and the other two Germans. They had arrived just in time to protect her because, he said sneeringly, it appeared that she was becoming involved in dangerous exploits that might bring her to harm. The whole tenor of his talk, the voice, the inflection, the choice of words, mocked her, taunted her, and infuriated her.

They carried her out of the house and to a waiting car. She tried to see where they were taking her, the direction they took from the abandoned house, but the Italian, with an exaggerated gesture, drew down the blinds in the back of the car and they drove through the darkened city as if she were in a private tunnel, seeing nothing. No one spoke for some time and then the Italian, addressing one of the men in the front seat, asked for a blindfold. It was handed over in silence, and while they rode on he folded the material across her eyes and fastened it securely around her head. In another few minutes she felt the car slow, almost to a stop, turn sharply and halt. There was grating of locks, the intermittent squeal of hinges, and they

94

moved forward again. Then stop. Car doors opening. Short, curt commands, both German and Italian, and she was taken bodily from the car and carried up, up a flight of long steps. From the clatter of the boots she guessed that the steps were stone; then suddenly they resounded on wood, and then were muffled in carpeting. In another moment she felt herself lowered into a chair; and the men who had been carrying her stepped back. Someone fumbled with the blindfold and slipped it quickly from her eyes.

Bright lights were flooding on to her, blinding her almost as effectively as the blindfold had done, and yet she could now make out the other figures in the room. Her Italian contact was standing before her leering at her with a twisted smile. Behind him the others, the two Germans and the other Italian, moved like shadows.

Fortunately, the binding and gagging and blindfolding of Gina had protected her more thoroughly than anything else could possibly have done. For it gave her time. Her rage, her mixed anger and terror when first she was seized in the abandoned house, most certainly would have prompted her to say things that she might later regret. As it was, unable to move or speak during the entire time between her capture and her arrival at the house, she had time to plan her strategy and develop her story. It would have to be good if she was to survive.

They began their questioning at once. The gag was removed and the ordeal began. One of the Germans drew up a small table and the other Italian, the one Gina had never seen before, seated himself at it, took out a small pad and a pen, and prepared to make notes. The contact, the Italian cut-out with whom Gina had been working for the Germans, strode importantly back and forth in the small room as he talked, posing questions, turning quickly to catch her out in an inaccuracy of time or place, needling her with inferences of a more complete knowledge of her actions than he very likely had. He accused her bluntly of working for the Allied services. This she denied as bluntly, looking him straight in the eye. He asked who her contact was, how long she had worked with him, what he had asked of her, and dozens of other questions. Gina answered them all quietly, cooperatively.

Then, when the time appeared right for it, she played her trump. Acidly, she accused them of bungling, of interfering with her mission. She was, she said with conviction, or at least she "hoped" she was making contact with an Allied agent on the chance that he might be useful. But of course now it was possible that they had spoiled her act by their stupid intervention. Supposing he had had her followed. Supposing he had seen her enter the abandoned house only to be carried out moments later by four men and spirited away in a car with drawn blinds. The man she was meeting was known to her only as Alfredo. She thought, but did not know, that he was in a position to make contact with Allied intelligence sources. But he was skittish. He had appeared to her to be highly nervous, and he did not know that she was a woman. If he became suspicious, if he had had her tailed, he would be lost to them forever as a source. And looking directly at her Italian contact she announced that she would inform the young Nazi counter-intelligence officer in Rome if for any reason such as this stupid interference her mission should be aborted.

It was a bold move. As she talked she thought that she could see a certain uneasiness in the men around her, and yet they kept at her with questions until long after the day had broken. Finally they left her alone, still bound.

There was a flat, hard-looking bed in the room, a washstand, two straight chairs other than the one in which she was seated, and one small window high in the wall. It was barred with a heavy grille. She longed for bed and finally, shuffling and half hopping on her bound feet, she made it from the chair and fell prostrate across the mattress. In a matter of minutes she had fallen into exhausted sleep, still bound, still dressed in a man's clothing.

Gina lost all concept of time. How long she had slept, what day it was, she found she could no longer remember, and what was in a way frightening, she found that she really didn't care what day it was, what time it was. She lay on the bed and wondered if she had been drugged, and yet they had offered her nothing to eat or drink, there had been no injections. Her hands, still bound behind her back, were numb and there was a dull ache the length of her arms and into her shoulders. Her feet were equally numb and there was a noticeable swelling around her ankles. She fought the pain and the numbness by filling her mind with plans. She recalled in detail what she had told her questioners during the first interrogation so that its repetition was almost automatic. Any slip, any slight varia-

96

tion in her story now would mean more pressure, torture, the discovery of her true position as a double agent, and certainly death. She felt that she had made a strong beginning. Now it was up to her to carry it forward, to insist, to convince, and to secure her release.

Suddenly she heard the lock on the door being worked and then two German guards came into the room. They came quickly over to the bed, and while one placed a blindfold again over her eyes the other released the cords that bound her ankles. They raised her to a sitting position and then released the bindings on her wrists. She thanked them and rubbed her hands, pulled at her prickling fingers, flexed them, and worked her shoulders and arms until she could feel the circulation begin to start. Her feet were dead to her until she put weight on them, and then they felt as if they had been pierced by thousands of needles probing deep into her legs. She stood only for a moment and then sat quickly again on the bed, rubbing her legs, swinging them from the knees.

One of the Germans spoke to her in ungrammatical, peculiarily guttural Italian, telling her that she would soon get the circulation going if she walked. They had come, he explained, to take her to the lavatory. She was bursting with discomfort, and she rose immediately and went with them. They escorted her, still blindfolded, down a long corridor and into a bathroom. They closed the door and then removed the blindfold from her eyes. There were the usual fixtures, and one of the Germans indicated the toilet. She thanked him and waited for him to leave the room. He stepped back against the door, took out a pack of cigarettes, and offered one to the other German standing beside him. He took one and they both concerned themselves with the lighting of their cigarettes, making no move to leave her to the privacy of the toilet.

Gina was equal to the embarrassment. She shrugged, turned to the toilet, undid her trousers and dropped them as would any man, and sat on the seat. The two Germans stood by the door stoically smoking and muttering small talk to each other. When she had finished and arranged her clothing, she went to the washbowl and scrubbed. She dashed cold water into her face and let the freshness linger in her eyes. And while she was washing one of the Germans nonchalantly strode to the toilet bowl, opened his fly, and urinated loudly. He belched and then broke wind with a loud report, and the second German spoke a mock apology. It suddenly struck Gina that they had not for a moment suspected that she was a woman. As she told it later, it was in some way a minor accolade.

They blindfolded her again before they led her from the bathroom. Then, back in her room, they removed the blindfold and re-bound her hands and feet. They locked the door behind them when they left.

Later in the day a guard brought her food. There was plenty of it, and there was wine to go with it, and she ate and drank heartily, not knowing or caring whether or not there were drugs in it. When she had finished, her hands were again tied behind her back and she was left to doze in discomfort on the bed.

It was dark in the room when next she heard the lock worked, the door quickly opened and closed and locked again. She pretended to be asleep, and she heard a man come over to the bed and stand quietly for a minute looking down at her. When he spoke, it was the voice of the Italian cut-out, her contact in the German service. She had always hated him, she knew that now, she had hated him from the first time she had seen him, hated him and distrusted him. And now that he had her completely at his mercy, completely under his control, she hated with an intensity that could easily bring her to murder. If only she had the chance, and the means.

He turned on a dim light in a corner of the small room and then came back to the bed. He wanted to admire her disguise as a man, he told her. It was such an admirable disguise. There was sneer and taunt, threat and menace, in his tone and she made no reply.

He sat on the edge of the bed and began to open her clothing. She struggled to fight him off, cursed at him, and began to scream. Roughly he stuffed his handkerchief into her mouth and, as if from nowhere, he produced a roll of tape and taped it into place. He was smiling, a leering, sickly smile as he worked on the gag, and when he had it securely in place he went on with the removal of her clothing. He opened her shirt front, tore away the undershirt, and ran his hands over her skin and breasts. He undid her belt, opened her trousers and slid them down to her knees, fondling her, caressing her as he did so.

He kept telling her that it was a clever disguise, that she had done it well. Then he rose, went to the side of the room and removed his own clothing. When he turned toward her he was nude, aroused and slaveringly lecherous. There was only one thing wrong with her disguise, she was lacking only one thing in her portrayal of a man, he said mockingly. He would correct that now, he said, he would give her the one thing she lacked.

Then he raped her.

The next few days were a living hell. Her clothing was taken from her and she was left completely nude in the small room, damp and cold. They left her unbound, and they came often to interrogate, to taunt, and to molest her with indecencies she couldn't bear to describe. And yet they couldn't break her story.

They tried the torture of immersion in first a scalding tub of water and then a quick plunge into ice water and then back again to the scalding water until they had to gag her again to muffle her screams. They drugged her with "truth" serums until she was almost insensate, retaining only wit enough to say nothing, and yet not knowing how she managed to fight it off. Still she clung to the story that she was actually developing her mission for the German service when they intercepted her.

Insistently she demanded that she be permitted to talk with the Nazi counterintelligence officer who had first recruited her. And each time she had made the demand there had been a noticeable uneasiness among her tormentors. Then, suddenly, one day he was there. He was the height of courtesy. In spotless uniform and with glistening boots, he demanded at once that she be given a robe to cover herself. He asked if she had been fed, and then ordered food and drink brought to her. He toyed with a glass of wine as she ate, and he talked with her of her mission. His manner was easy, relaxed, friendly, almost casual, a trifle too disarming. Gina was on guard.

She told him again the story that she had first told the Italian cut-out. She insisted that they had perhaps ruined what might have been a successful and rewarding mission. Beyond salvage no doubt by now, she shrugged.

The Nazi officer listened to her quietly.

She used every bit of charm at her command. She focused her large dark eyes on him intently and she talked with an intense sincerity, for this was for her very life. She told him that she could prove herself if she could be given a chance.

She would again contact the man Alfredo. She would arrange with them ahead of time so that they could shadow her, but they must guarantee that they would not make any move to seize the man. It was, she insisted, an important contact, and they would spoil all of her work if they should interfere now. All she needed was trust. The large dark eyes watched and waited.

The Nazi was silent a long time. But when he spoke, it was to say that he had confidence in her; that he believed her; that she would be given a chance to prove herself.

Gina listened in a trance, hardly believing what she heard, and there was a long silence between them when he had finished speaking. Then she leaned forward and took his hand and squeezed it in hers.

He slept with her that night.

"After all," she told us disarmingly, "I really loved him at the moment. And why not, he saved my life."

Gina never knew where the house in which she had been held for those terrifying days and night was located. For when at last she was released to pursue her mission, she was once again blindfolded in her room, led to the car and driven, still blindfolded, back to the abandoned house where they had first captured her. The Nazi counterintelligence officer was with them when they let her out of the car late one night, and he assured her that he would remain in Naples until she had had time to contact Alfredo and continue her mission.

Everything now had changed. Most certainly she would be shadowed, constantly, eternally shadowed in everything she did. The important thing was not to panic. She must not, she cautioned herself over and over, do anything to tip her hand, to show that she was uncertain. Every move she made, from here on out, had to be made with confidence. One false step, one slight display of nerves, and she knew what the consequences would be. She would be liquidated. But only after rigorous interrogation and the attendant tortures the Nazis had perfected with an insane sadism.

Two days later, with the full knowledge of the Nazi counter-intelligence officer and the Italian cut-out, Gina made contact with the man she had identified to them as Alfredo. He was waiting for her in a crowded, stinking, smoke-filled waterfront café. It was noisy; there was loud talk and laughter, crude talk and the tight, explosive feeling that trouble, riot, sudden violence, and murder lay just under the surface of the phony camaraderie. Gina had been there before and she had become hardened to it, but she always wondered what would happen if it were discovered that, under the soiled cap, the tattered, worn, and misshapen coat, sweater, and trousers, standing in the heavy boots, was not just another drifting male but a woman.

Fortunately, with the shrewd foresight of the professional agent, Gina had long since worked out the code for just such a situation as now confronted them. Alfredo was seated on a stool at the end of a bar. He had placed a duffle bag on the stool next to him to save it for her, and as she walked toward him a cigarette, bent and crumpled, hung from the left corner of her mouth. It was unlighted. It told Alfredo what he needed to know, that they were being tailed.

They exchanged casual, loud-friendly greetings, and Alfredo bought a drink for her, shouting his order above the din. Not a motion, not a glance, not a tone to indicate that he knew now that he was in peril, that they both were in immediate danger. Gina lighted the cigarette, inhaled deeply, and reached for her glass. He raised his, they touched and then drank in silence. Her back was to the room, and she made the most of it. Alfredo made loud small talk, but her replies were lower key, and they were deadly earnest. She told him quickly that she was suspect, that their present meeting was a test, that she was sure she could carry on only a short time longer. Alfredo was wonderful. He laughed as if she were telling some bawdy joke, but he was careful to catch every word she said.

She would arrange one more meeting with him, and he must not fail her. It would have to be a shadowed one. She would have to tell the Germans of it, let them in on time and place of rendezvous. She felt it was her final chance to bring off her deception of the Germans. Her life, his life, the success of the mission depended upon it. He would have to be ready for a trap, she warned him, and she was sure she would have to go into hiding for a time, no matter what happened. Provided she *could* go into hiding at this point, provided she could elude the shadow the Germans had placed on her.

She set the time, the place, and the date of the rendezvous. It would be five days from then.

She asked him if he had any information, preferably something in writing, that she could take back with her to the German service. It would help strengthen her position. It was imperative to ensure the success of the scheme she had just arranged with him.

Alfredo laughed again and, still chuckling, he opened his duffel bag and rummaged through it. He pulled out spare socks, a soiled shirt, some underclothes, making an open display of the action. At last he found what he was looking for, a fat, black, old-fashioned fountain pen. He pulled out some rumpled bits of paper from a pocket and made a tick-tack-toe graph, made the first X and passed it to Gina. She took the pen, made an O and passed the paper back. They both laughed, and under his breath he told her to pocket the pen when they had finished the game. They played three or four games, paid up their small bets, drained their glasses, and said good-bye.

Gina swaggered from the café with a purely feigned gusto. Beneath the bravado, beneath the hunched shoulders and the rolling walk, her heart was thumping wildly, her whole body was trembling, and she could feel the hot flush that reddened her face. The cool damp of the air outside came as a stimulant.

This was the most dangerous time of all. This would be the moment of the double cross. The Nazi counterintelligence officer had given his word that they would not try to take Alfredo. But she had never been sure. The Germans, every one of them, were treacherous, and she felt, deep down, that they would never let him get away, that their acceptance of her plan was only a ruse, that they would move in on them both, Alfredo and herself, and that would be the end. She had expected it every moment while they were together in the café. And it hadn't happened. Now, walking quickly from the café to her prearranged rendezvous with the Nazi and the Italian, she was still apprehensive. It could be now. They could have already taken him, waited until she had left, grabbed him without her knowledge, and then they would take her and he would never know. She saw the whole pattern. The interrogation, in separate rooms, each one not knowing what the other had said or was saying. The tortures, the ceaseless, ever more cruel, ever more brutal tortures, until every drop of information, every drop of blood, had been squeezed from them. She pressed on, inwardly filled with the fear that she was walking into a trap yet determined to conquer that fear.

She reviewed again her whole story, and it gave her confidence. The fact that the Italian had stopped his torture and his questioning, had met her demand, and had called in the Nazi counterintelligence officer, his superior, was in her favour; this showed that her plan was working. The Nazi's belief in her, their quick, wholly physical but rather pleasant romance, this helped. And finally there was his word that they would do nothing to spoil her contact with Alfredo.

One further thing made her sure that the tightwire she was walking would hold her. The Nazi was too clever an operative to move in at once on someone like Alfredo, even if he didn't believe her story. It would be infinitely more profitable to the German service to let them play along together, Gina and Alfredo, and then to pick them up after they had perhaps led to other contacts. On this Gina staked her life.

There was more confidence in her stride now, and she was calmed, in control of her emotions when they picked her up. Several blocks from the café, the car slid slowly along the kerb, a door opened, and she was inside. In another moment they were racing out of the city to a hideout she had known nothing about. It was isolated, a small farmhouse, and it gave no indication to the casual observer of the sinister purpose it was serving.

It was there, in the secluded farmhouse, that Gina took out the fountain pen that Alfredo had given her. She unscrewed the barrel that held the ink sac and tapped the pen against her finger. A slender, tightly packed roll of thin tissue slid from the barrel on to the table in front of her. There were several bits, each one containing a message. It was intelligence concerning the Allied troops. And all of it, unknown to the Germans, had been carefully screened and planted by the OSS for the benefit of German-Italian confusion.

There was a map diagram of a projected landing in a highly vulnerable area. There were statistics on air losses, supply shortages, and resistance problems. There was even a lovely rumour that Hitler had been liquidated by an inner circle of the Nazi hierarchy, that it was being kept from the German people and especially the troops, until the new clique in power could arrange proper surrender terms. This bit caused much comment and a certain amount of concern among the assembled group of Nazi operatives. It rather dampened their enthusiasm for the success of Gina's work.

They studied the other reports carefully. They were heartened by the evidence that the partisans were causing the Allies some headaches. They agreed that the map of the projected landing should be sent on as quickly as possible by messenger to the proper headquarters command.

Most important, they admitted that Gina had been highly successful in her contact with Alfredo and that she should continue to see him.

At least for the time being.

Five days later Gina kept her rendezvous with Alfredo.

It was, of course, done with the knowledge and the consent of the Nazi counterintelligence officer. And though she was fully aware of the dangers involved, fully aware that perhaps this time the Germans would move in on her and take Alfredo with her, she was working with confidence.

She had not wasted the five days. Constantly, she had planned and schemed with the Nazis as to how best to exploit this contact she had with the man Alfredo. Perhaps he would work for them, perhaps he could open new contacts deeper in the Allied services, perhaps he could even get her a job, an open job, in some strategic spot in the Allied command. The Nazi's dream of the possibilities were endless, and Gina felt a sudden ironic pleasure in his choice of the word "strategic". By the time the day had arrived, she had him so excited with the potentials of her mission she was filled with assurance.

Gina had arranged the rendezvous for mid-afternoon in the very busiest part of Naples. She had deliberately chosen the daylight hours and the crowded streets as a protection from a possible double cross by the Germans. Further, if for any reason the plan should abort, if Alfredo should fail her, it would be better to be able to melt into the crowds and perhaps elude her German shadows. She would be on her own again, and again suspect. It would be helpful to gain as much time as possible before facing the Nazi with an explanation.

She moved confidently through the crowded streets. The day was bright but cold, and there was no sauntering, none of the dawdling stroll and gape the Italians so love. Everyone moved with intent.

Gina had her cap pulled well down on her head, her hands were thrust deep into her trousers pockets, her shoulders were hunched. She knew the area well, and she could approach the rendezvous with complete nonchalance. She would make no effort to locate Alfredo. It was perhaps half a block, and she decided that it was for him to make the contact, for him to make the move. She would be at the proper place at the proper time. The rest was up to him.

A couple of police were coming toward her, moving with the crowd, doing a beat. She only noticed them without really registering. She had long since trained herself to accept the threat of the police. Her papers were in order; that was always the main thing with the police. She carried the papers of the dead young Italian, the papers that went with the clothes and, though she had seldom been asked to produce them, she had almost begun to think of herself by his name. At least when she was wearing his clothes. It was a taken-for-granted thing.

They came closer, the police, and then suddenly there they were, directly in front of her, blocking her way, asking to see her papers. She brought out her identity card, her work card, her police registration. They were tattered and worn from much handling. The police looked at them all carefully. First one policeman, then the other, each one scanned each bit of paper in frowning silence. They asked her one or two questions, listened carefully to her answers, and spoke asides to each other. People, dozens, scores of people passed them by, uninvolved, unconcerned—if aware at all, only to the extent of being grateful that the police had not stopped them.

Then one of the police said that it would perhaps be well if she came with them for further questioning. Something about her papers. He was polite, and he took her by the arm and walked with her in the direction she had been going. The other policeman, also holding an arm, walked on the other side of her.

Her first impulse was to run, to tear away, to run for her life from this new threat. And yet the whole incident had happened so quickly, so unexpectedly, a sudden overwhelming fear seemed to turn her legs to jellied encumbrances. She protested that she had done nothing, that her papers were in order, that she was on her way to work and would be late for her job. The police listened in silence, without comment, and walked her along between them through the crowds. At the end of the block they turned a corner into a side street, as noisy and as crowded as the one they had been on, and they walked along, pace for pace, in silence.

A police car was coming toward them down the street, and

one of the police escorting her, with a kind of surprised pleasure at the good luck, hailed the driver. The car pulled to the kerb, and the officer who had hailed it went over and spoke a few words to the driver. He then opened the door to the back and motioned Gina and the other policeman to get in. He climbed in beside them, and the car moved off down the street, not at speed but normally, working with the traffic.

Gina thought of Alfredo. She wondered if he had seen her at all, wondered if he would ever know what had happened to her. She thought of the Nazi counterintelligence officer, of her shadow, and she wondered if they had seen her being questioned by the police, if they could in some way come to her rescue. Hundreds of related thoughts spiralled in her brain, building toward panic, and she fought them with sheer force of will. She thought ahead to her prospective questioning at police headquarters. She would remain calm. She would not lose her temper and rail at them. She would cooperate and it would be routine, she would be given back her papers, she would be released and, perhaps, just possibly, she would still be able to make the rendezvous with Alfredo.

The car rounded a corner, went a few yards down the street, and then stopped before huge double doors. The driver blew his horn once, the doors opened to a courtyard, and they drove on in while the doors closed behind them. There was another car in the courtyard, and the police car pulled alongside of it and stopped.

The next few moments were like an explosion. In a matter of seconds Gina was pushed from the police car into the one waiting alongside and told to lie flat on the floor in the back. Ask no questions, one of the police told her, just do as you are told, if you want to live. Someone threw a rug over her and then she felt things piled on top, either light crates or cardboard cartons, two, perhaps three. She had hardly had time to see who else was in the car with her, only to note that there were two young men, plainly dressed, in the front seat. They were talking quietly, rapidly, to each other, to the police, to her, a jumble of confusing, frightening words in Italian staccato. There was no time, no chance to resist. She could only comply.

In another moment the car moved forward in the courtyard, the huge doors opened again, and they were in the street. From the starting and stopping of the car she could tell that they were not rushing, that they were driving at normal city speed. Then there was acceleration, slowings and stoppings were fewer, and they drove for what seemed an hour on rough roads. There was no conversation between the two men in the front, and no one suggested that she might come out from under her blanket, that she might sit up in the car. The cold bite of the weather made her content to stay snuggled under the rug, warm, dark, protected.

The road was rougher now, so they were driving more slowly. Then, slowing, halt, start again, drive a short distance, and stop.

Someone opened the door to the back. She heard them lift the crates or boxes, felt the release of their slight weight. They pulled away the rug.

"You can get out now."

Alfredo helped her from the car.

It was like being in another world, the OSS hideout south of Naples. The little stone house, the tranquil view, the quiet, the food, the beds, the baths. Gina revelled in it all. She soaked in tubs of hot water; she slept in clean fresh beds, free of the apprehension, the stark terror of so many nights in Naples; she ate heartily and well. Days of this, only indolence, calm and quiet, before anything was said or discussed of her mission. Time to gain composure, time to freshen the spirit, time to rest the body, this was what she needed, and this is what she was offered.

Then and only then did Alfredo talk with her of her further assignment, where they should go from here. He was pleased that his "arrest" of Gina had worked so smoothly, and yet, try as she might, Gina could not get him to tell her how it was all done. She never found out, for instance, whether the police were bona-fide Naples policemen cooperating with the OSS, or whether they were OSS agents impersonating Italian police. Either way it was exciting. She never found out whether the change from one car to another was actually done in the courtyard of a police precinct station or in some OSS address. All she could discover was that Alfredo was so sure of the success of his plan he had never even gone into Naples to keep the rendezvous and risk his own capture. The whole plan had been so carefully detailed in advance he knew that all he would have to do would be to await Gina's arrival at the OSS area south of Naples.

But what of the Nazi counterintelligence officer and the shadow Gina had left in Naples? She and Alfredo speculated on their reactions. They laughed over the possible confrontation of the Naples police by German authorities protesting at the arrest of an Italian citizen. Even if they dared, it would make an amusing spectacle. And, as Gina pointed out, if the police had not been accomplices, if they had been impersonated by OSS agents, the whole possible scene was of Gilbert and Sullivan proportions, the protesting Germans being more convinced of Italian guilt the more the Italian police protested innocence.

All that remained now was for them to solidify the plans for Gina's return to Naples and to build her story and evidence that she had been kidnapped by Allied intelligence agents as a German spy. It would have to be airtight if she was to be able to continue with the confidence of the Nazi counter-intelligence officer. They spent a couple of weeks on it, Alfredo and Gina, and then she was ready to go back.

After the soft dresses and the leisured life of the OSS hide-out, it was hard to get back into the tattered, dirty apparel of the dead Italian and go back to the masquerade of being a man. But it was deemed the only safe way for her to get back into Naples. She insisted on it herself, and she insisted on making her own way, the OSS giving her a lift only to get her out of the immediate area of the hideout.

One other decision had been made that saddened her. There would be no more contact with Alfredo. He could never again be placed in a position of surveillance by the Germans without running the risk of capture, torture, and death. Further, the pure logic of it was self-evident. If Alfredo had been the instigator of her seizure by the Allied forces, how could she continue to operate with him, in the eyes of the German service, without running the same risk again? Or worse, how could she convince the Germans that she was their own agent, and still meet with a man who had kidnapped her? Alfredo assigned her another contact.

Gina reached Naples without any problems. She went first to the abandoned house and discovered that what few clothes she had left there had vanished. There was nothing. It meant that she would have to abandon this hideout. For, if the Germans themselves had not taken all of her things, then it meant that some other vagabond had discovered the vacant house and she would no longer be able to use it with safety.

She went on to the *pensione* where she had been maintaining a room. The landlady didn't recognize her in her male disguise, and when she identified herself she was told that someone had come a few days previously, had paid up her rent, released her room, and taken all of her things. It was an Italian gentleman, the landlady said, and he told her that Gina had moved into another apartment.

This was disturbing news, and she took a bit of time figuring out what she should do next. She found a room in a cheap hotel and then, after a day to get her bearings, she made contact with the Italian cut-out. He was delighted to see her, filled with concern for her welfare; he plied her with innumerable questions. The Nazi counterintelligence officer would be glad to know that she had escaped. He had gone back to Rome, but he had left word that he was to be alerted the moment she returned. He wanted to see her as soon as possible.

She was guarded. This could be either good or bad news, this reaction, the eagerness of the Nazi to see her.

When he arrived he wanted to hear everything. He told her the Italian police were corrupt, that they were no doubt, at least some of them, in the pay of the Allies and, when they had seen her arrested, when she vanished from sight, they were certain that she had been kidnapped on orders of the man Alfredo. You could never trust the damned Americans, he told her. They were deceitful, treacherous, and dangerous enemies for all of their naïveté.

He asked about the tortures they employed. He kept pressing her on this point, asking if they had any techniques unknown to the German services, if they kept her in solitary, if they tried starvation, if they used drugs, if they beat her. He wanted to know if they had abused her sexually, if they tried any "experiments" on her, and what kind of information they sought.

And he wanted to know how she had escaped.

Gina gave him the full treatment. She told him that she had been indeed captured by the Americans, that they had treated her as a suspected German spy, but they had treated her well. Yes, they had kept her confined, they had questioned her relentlessly, they were particularly interested in the German plans for fighting on in Italy. But they had not harmed her, they had not assaulted her sexually, and she had been well fed.

The Nazi was disappointed.

Then she went on to say that she had not escaped from the Americans. They had released her. She had managed to convince them that she was not a German spy, but a poor war widow, that she had lost two children as well as a husband to the war, that she was displaced. It was the whole cover story the Nazi himself had built for her. He listened enthralled, delighted to think that his ruse had worked, that he had in fact deceived the Americans, got a spy into their midst, and fooled them into releasing her. But then, he added, the Americans are so innocent, so soft, so trusting.

She had never seen Alfredo again, she told the Nazi. And she thought now that perhaps he had nothing to do with the Americans, that he might be working with another group, what she did not know. She had contacted him quite by chance, she told the Nazi; they had talked freely of the war, he had been pro-Allies, and she had pretended to go along with him. She felt he might have been trying to use her, to get her to work for him, and that explained his giving her the information he had as evidence of good faith. Or it could have been a snare. Somehow she felt Alfredo had had something to do with her capture. Perhaps he had given her the items in the pen as a plant, to be found on her when arrested, to ensure her liquidation. He did not know that she was a woman, as she had always been in her male disguise when she met him.

The Americans, on the other hand, knew that she was a woman. They had picked her up as a man, but they had soon found out her disguise. They had asked her to work for them. She watched the Nazi counterintelligence officer's reaction to this and, as he showed interest, as she saw him respond, she built her story. They would like to use her in the area, they could provide contacts, she was to let them know.

It worked.

He was delighted. Of course she should keep the contact. She should pretend to work for them. It would be a triumph for him, for German intelligence, if she could pretend to be spying for the Allies, for the Americans, all the while working for him. He was now convinced that Gina was potentially the greatest intelligence agent he had ever dealt with. He never knew how right he was.

He gave her assignments in the Naples area. Then, as the war advanced up the Italian boot, he withdrew her to Rome and operated her there for many months. More and more they placed confidence in her, until she was the key figure in the principal network being run by the Germans in Rome. He encouraged, he fostered, her contact with Allied personnel without question until, as Gina said, she could have held an open meeting with General Donovan himself and the Nazi would have smiled, nodded with smug assurance, and congratulated her on her cleverness.

She got us almost everything we wanted to know. And in many cases a lot more. She had access to much of the most secret of Nazi intelligence and, more important, the super-secret reports of the military and the air force, the naval forces and the like, which backed up the intelligence material.

The Germans were liberal, so great was her success with them, and they provided her with ample funds "for the subversion of Allied agents and for bribes". Dollars and pounds sterling were the favoured currencies for this, and they poured them out to her for use. They would have been horrified had they known that the same dollars and pounds were sent on to London to us as an extra dividend, unexpected but welcome. And many of them went on to be used for our purposes against the Germans. It was a mad merry-go-round.

Gina had one last frightening episode before the war ended. As the Germans retreated from Rome and the Allies came in, Gina was left behind for the purpose of further espionage service. And in the mad scramble of occupation she was picked up by the American forces as a suspected German operative. She was held, questioned, and examined, and they discovered the telltale code number tattooed on her left heel by the Germans. It was a damning and frightening bit of evidence that could have ended in disaster. Gina insisted that the American military authorities contact OSS London for verification of her status.

Franco had been loyal. We had the German code properly filed away with Gina's records. It was as Franco had sent it, and it was identified as having been placed on her heel *and* on the inner surface of her right buttock. This latter the Americans had overlooked.

It was November 1945. It was London.

Gina had been flown out of Italy sometime in early October, and she had been relaxing at one of the OSS rest areas in the English countryside. I had got most of her story over a period of days. Now she was preparing to go back to Italy.

We dined quietly at the Connaught, Gina and I, after the theatre, and she was gay, softly feminine, the very antithesis of the tough partisan fighter, the cunning double agent I knew her to be. It had left no mark, this horrid tale, I remember thinking that evening as we talked. Now it was all a lark, a kind of super-spy story that one had gone through in a trance, not touched by it, just slightly disturbed as by a nasty nightmare.

She had served as a double agent for the Office of Strategic Services for a span of almost nineteen months. Every moment of that time she had lived with deception and treachery, literally a whisper, a motion, a glance away from discovery, torture, and death. It had left no visible mark.

If she referred at all to her service that evening, it was only to recall the amusing things that had happened. Her first encounter with a men's room; her "kidnapping" by the police; her wonderful flow of dollars and pounds from the Germans, sent on to us. There was no mention of the other bits. And one can only guess at the things she had left unsaid, buried forever out of her memory.

She talked of the future. She was leaving the next day for Italy, and she wondered what she would find in the post-war years. Her longing was the longing of all the young who have been exposed to war, for a peaceful, free existence in a world at last gone sane. Of one thing she was certain. Whatever the future held for her, it would be unexciting after what she had seen and done during the war.

To that I agreed.

I watched her as she talked, and for some reason I thought ahead, way ahead, thirty, forty years, trying to picture Gina as an old lady, perhaps with grandchildren. I could see her with perhaps one on each knee saying, "Granny, tell us what the war was like." And I laughed to myself at the picture of the little old lady telling her grandchildren of these things she had done, the horrors she had endured. And they would all think she had gone mad, that Granny was dotty.

She saw me smiling and asked why.

I told her, and she laughed at the picture herself. Then, suddenly, the smile vanished and she became thoughtful.

"These things one would never tell children." She paused. "These things one would never tell anyone. That is—never anyone who hadn't been mixed up in it. Nobody would believe it."

She fingered the large diamond, emerald, and sapphire clip she was wearing. It was the one that had belonged to the old Italian woman she had impersonated, someone she had never known, given to her by the enemy.

"Would you believe how I got this clip?" Her dark eyes were steadily on me. "If you didn't know?"

Gina took off for Italy by air the next day. There were three others with her. They never got there, and no one is sure that the plane was ever found. The next spring, high in the Alps, some wreckage was spotted, but nothing could be done about it.

CHAPTER THREE

THE SPONSOR

THE Office of Strategic Services operated in almost every corner of the world throughout the war. There was a complicated and vast network of espionage and sabotage operations in every country of Europe. The Scandinavian countries, the Balkans, the Iberian Peninsula, the Middle East, and North Africa. We were there.

Then, as the war spread to the Far East, there was the need for further expansion of operations into areas unfamiliar and remote. India, Burma, Ceylon, Malaya, Assam, Thailand, and China, we were there as well. Even on into Japan. These were assignments of tremendous complexity. And by comparison they made operations within the European theatre seem simple and routine.

In the first place, from a long association with immigrant groups and their assimilation into the American scene, we were off to a head start in our operations in the European countries. Not only did we have a pool of solidly reliable Americans with intimate knowledge of European countries and people. We had a vast reservoir of American-born citizens from first-generation European stock, still aware of the customs, the attitudes, even the language of the stock from which they came. It meant that there were many possible recruits for the dangerous and tedious, lonely and thankless espionage and sabotage assignments.

There was an even more important factor that tipped the balance in favour of the European area. It was the Caucasian as against the Oriental individual. Many old-line Americans, provided they had the language facility, could melt easily into the European background. Obviously, the French-American, the Italian-American, the Scandinavian-American, all of the national mixtures could easily be infiltrated into the proper area for effective work. They had the physical characteristics.

But where did one find Americans who could pass as Burmese, Chinese, Malayan, or Japanese? Where were the mixtures, the Burmese-Americans, the Chinese-Americans, the Malay-Americans, the Japanese-Americans? They were practically nonexistent. And even where they did exist, as with the Nisei on the West Coast, the government dared not take a chance with them and herded them into restricted camps for the duration. It made the clandestine work of an organization like the Office of Strategic Services almost hopelessly complex.

Those were the basics. And if they were not enough hindrance to our progress in the war, there was a purely administrative man-made roadblock. It was the adamant position taken by General MacArthur in his refusal to permit the OSS to operate in any area under his command.

The ordinary individual, faced with such staggering odds, would have turned away from the idea of any sizeable clandestine operation in the Far East. But General Donovan was not an ordinary individual. The patently impossible was to him only a challenge, something infinitely more desirable to attack than the routinely possible. He was the perfect example of the type who took to heart that old cliché that was hung over many a war desk: "The possible we do immediately; the impossible takes a little longer."

So the OSS invaded the Far East. Main bases, discreetly camouflaged as to their real purpose, were established in India, Ceylon, Malaya, Burma, Thailand, Assam, and China. And like the multiplication of the amoeba, small hidden units split off from the larger bases until there were countless little nests of espionage and sabotage operatives in all of the major areas of the Far East.

British assistance was essential in the first stages. With the blessing of Prime Minister Churchill, General Orde Wingate and Lord Mountbatten were tremendously cooperative in aiding General Donovan with the necessary clearances in an area of British influence. Then, in our own services, General "Vinegar Joe" Stilwell took to the OSS with enormous enthusiasm. But from there on, every assignment, every small gain, every scrap of success had to be clawed from the country involved in the most painstaking manner.

Every espionage and sabotage assignment calls for impro-visation, for "playing by ear". In the Far East it could quite truthfully be said that every step leading up to the preparation of every mission called for the same. And where the average assignment called for nerve and courage in super-human doses, the Far Eastern assignments called also for tact, adaptability, and diplomacy of incredible delicacy.

David's mission was a case in point. Perhaps more bizarre, certainly more delicate and personal than most, it is the per-fect example of the unexpected extremes to be encountered in espionage and sabotage.

David was the most unlikely prospect, when one studies his background, for the type of operation he encountered in the OSS. He was the typical young American. From a Mid-western family, he had early had heavy responsibility placed on him. His father had died when he was fourteen and had left him with a younger brother and sister to be cared for along with his mother. It was the usual melancholy situation. While the father was living, there was a certain family well-being, a solid financial stability. Not a rich family, not a poor family, but like so many thousands of families, living well as long as the head of the house was there and producing. But once the main prop is gone there is near-disaster. It is then that the real testing of an individual, no matter the age, is made.

David met the test. He got work after school hours. He took extra work during vacations and, with what his mother could bring in from part-time work, he was able to keep the family going. He tried to get a full education for himself, but as his brother and sister came along and more funds were needed for their schooling, he left in his second year of college and took a full-time, well-paying job that had been offered to him.

From that it was the Army and the war.

The OSS got hold of David through the incessant process of screening the thousands of officer candidates available to the army. His record was good, he had shown high averages on all of his army ratings, and there was coupled with the energy and ability a pleasant personality, a certain charm, and an attractive person. He came to us as a lieutenant.

All of this he had, but he could hardly have been called worldly, a sophisticate in the correct sense of the term. Travel had been denied him because of the circumstances of his youth. He had had practically no exposure to new and different cultures, nationalities, manners, and customs. An inbred interest in the arts and music had been fostered as much as possible, but it had not really broadened him to an understanding of the world. He was a provincial. A good, clean-cut, earnest, solid and sincere American provincial, but still a provincial for all that.

General Donovan was building up the operational units for the Far East. He was asking for young men with imagination, with the natural aggressiveness to tackle any situation with assurance, and the ability and nerve to carry it through without regard for "normal" procedures. As he had so often said, "I'd rather have a young Lieutenant with guts enough to disobey an order than a Colonel too regimented to think and act for himself."

David presented himself for consideration. His natural manner, his American good looks, his easy charm, and above all his enthusiasm and assurance that he could handle anything thrown at him, impressed the General. He was sent to India.

To anyone with a passing familiarity with India the problems facing this young man should be evident. The word most frequently used in connection with India is "teeming", and it is expressive and apt. Everything in India is teeming. The hordes of people, ragged, bedraggled, starving, listlessly filthy. The hordes of taboos, the limitless sects, the endless rites, religious beliefs, castes—nowhere in the world is it less possible to generalize about a people and their customs than in India. One group will eat no flesh where another will eat no fish. Some eschew all pork, others insist on eating in strict privacy. Some believe in a rigidly observed celibacy, others indulge the senses in rites that go beyond the erotic into the indecent, obscene, and degrading. How does one adjust to a country where there can be the magnificent, oppressive luxury of the maharajahs and the slow starvation of millions? How does one react to the religious sect so devout as to spend every waking hour in silent contemplation while, at the other end of the scale, is a sect observing religious rites so degrading as to include the eating of offal and excrement? What does one do with tribal groups who sanction and practise female infanticide; others that practise child marriages even at the almost-infant age of four, and still others to whom marriage is so important they will sanction marriage to a flower rather than permit a daughter to go through life without a "husband"? And how does the Western mind accept the practice of cremating the living widow on the funeral pyre of her husband; the mystical reverence of the sacred cows; the worship and protection of endless tribes of monkeys? How does one adjust to the idea that there are "untouchables", people so loathed in the rigid social scale of caste they must call out their approach to permit others not to be contaminated by contact with them?

Teeming? A country so burdened is also seething, wretchedly, one might almost say hopelessly, seething with complexes beyond comprehension to the average Westerner.

David was plummeted into this rolling maelstrom. It was his mission to recruit, organize, and train native personnel as saboteurs for the OSS to be used against the Japanese wherever they might be most vulnerable. Written, like this, it looks neat, tidy, and quite simple. In fact it involved complexities beyond all imagining.

Fortunately, out of all this bewildering mass of human contradictions, two things played into David's hands. The first was the fact that, owing to the long association with the British, an unusually high percentage of the natives of whatever faith or tribal connection spoke English. The other fact was that one tribe alone stood out as warriors. The Gurkhas, above all others in India, had the longest history, the proudest record as fighters of incredible courage and daring, inhuman ferocity and tenacity. It would be among the proud Gurkhas that he would be most likely to discover the men he needed for the sabotage activities of the OSS.

From their earliest colonial days in India, the British had recognized the high quality of the Gurkha warriors as fighting men. And if one looks back in British history, one will discover Gurkha regiments serving the British Crown in almost every major military operation. There were Gurkha troops who distinguished themselves in the First World War under British command. There were equally proud regiments activated and tremendously valuable to the British in the Second World War. Several years ago the British government officially recognized the importance of the Gurkhas when the King of Nepal was made an honorary field marshal in the British

Army in gratitude for the Gurkha soldiers he had provided the Crown. It was the first time such an honour had been granted.

OSS headquarters in New Delhi found a small house for David. It was well situated, back from the travelled highway, and in a small garden of its own. It had been built and occupied formerly by a British businessman, and it had comfort and amenities expected by the Westerner. But it was also accessible enough to be useful in the interviewing and recruitment of the personnel he sought.

First of all he needed a "boy". In India a "boy" can be literally a boy, perhaps of fourteen or more, or he can be a bent, semi-crippled man of seventy. Whatever his age, he is the indispensable body servant without which no one can accomplish anything. A good "boy" does everything but breathe for one. He runs errands, he acts as cook-butler-valet, confidant, nurse. He sleeps just outside the door to one's room on a mat like a dog. And, in most cases, once the attachment is made, he stays with one until death.

So installed, in a house of his own, with a personal boy, two other servants besides, and the necessary organization and money of the OSS behind him, David was in a world as far removed from the one in which he had grown up as it would be possible to imagine.

One other change was made. David was elevated to the rank of captain. The importance of his mission demanded that he should make contact with men in authority, men who could say yes to him and make it stick. And the Eastern World, perhaps as status-conscious as the American society has become, the prestige of rank was a tangible asset.

The first few weeks were filled with frustrations. Contacts were made, discussions were held, there was much formality; there were bowings and smiles, toasts drunk, meals proffered, but there was little actual progress made. Always there was the polite agreement that help *could* be provided, but then the discussion bogged down in the details. No one seemed to be able to give the final word. It was a maddening experience.

Then, quite unexpectedly one evening over a drink with a Gurkha officer, casual mention was made of the fact that there was a man of great power, a Gurkha chieftain, who would perhaps be able to help. But he lived far away. The Gurkhas, it was explained, were originally from Nepal, and some of their most powerful leaders were still there. They were men proud beyond all imagining, men who refused to come to the world, men who demanded that the world come to them. There was one such, the Gurkha officer explained to David, a chieftain, away in the remote reaches of Nepal, who, if the terms were right, just might. . . .

It took them two days to reach the Gurkha chieftain at the small enclave that made up his headquarters.

They had travelled by jeep: David, his "boy", the young Gurkha officer who had first suggested the plan, and his "boy". At first the roads were cluttered with the throngs that seem to be always on the move, always in motion, slow motion, in India. Holy men, beggars, women and children, they clogged the highways with a kind of aimlessness that made no sense. Most of them were on foot, but there were now and then fortunates who rode bicycles, others who jolted along in a type of two-wheeled wooden tumbril. It was invariably drawn by a slow-moving bullock, and it was usually piled high with the debris of marginal life, bales, bundles, baskets, the whole held down by as many people as could cling atop the crazy heap.

It was like travelling through Dante's Inferno. It was the raw, ugly, hideous, earthy basic of the human condition exposed totally. Emaciated women lay in the dust along the edge of the road and nursed equally emaciated children. At every turn someone was defecating or urinating into the ditch along the road, while only a pace or two away another might be rinsing his hands or laundering some pitiable rag in the same ditch. Some crouched like monkeys in the dirt and picked at scraps. Some sat and begged. Some indulged in sexual obscenities. Some lay wrapped in filthy rags and slept— though of this one could never be sure, because some lay dying and some were already dead, swollen and festering.

The sacred cows wandered everywhere, and there were those who followed them and collected their dung. They smeared it fresh-dropped into their hair and then dried the matted, stinking mass in the sun. Equally privileged with the sacred cows were the monkeys. They were everywhere, scavenging, stealing, fighting and fornicating, and consuming tons of food that could have gone to the feeding of these unfortunate people.

Nobody cared. This was the most appalling fact. All was accepted with a listless unconcern, a fatalistic acceptance that seemed untouched by feeling or compassion. The dead body caused no more concern lying in the ditch than would a banana peel. It made no difference.

And over it all, the stench. The stench of rot, of death. The stench of carrion, of excrement and urine. The stench of sweat, of the unbathed, of disease and mould. The very air seemed to David so fetid it was as if all of the disgusting odours of the world had been concentrated along this rough and dusty Indian road.

Mercifully, as they went on, the crowds seemed to thin, then the road became a lane, the lane became a track, and they were once again in a world that seemed, by contrast, washed, cool, green, and deliciously fragrant.

They spent the night in a former government rest house. Prior to the war it must have been a popular retreat for the British, but it was now run down. The rooms were high and stone-floored, cool and dark, but the heavy red Victorian hangings were tattered, the brass fittings were dulled, there was a dismal air of abandonment about the huge building. It wasn't helped by the fact that there seemed to be only a few other guests in the vast gloom.

It was here they left the jeep.

With two boys as bearers, David and the Gurkha officer made the rest of the trip on foot. There was no passable road to the domain of the Gurkha chieftain, but there was a well-marked and obviously much used trail. They were now in an area of deep gorges and high mountains, and the going was slow and strenuous. But it had its compensations in the scenery. It was wildly beautiful. Huge, dense forests, dark glades, sudden open clearings and breathtaking views, the rush of water, the colour of flowers and birds, it was so different from the morass he had so recently escaped it was beyond belief.

Then, as if by magic, the dense jungle growth was cleared and they were on a high plateau. It was neatly ordered, green, and serene, and there were many buildings, a kind of self-contained village set about a garden-like court. A large house of brick-red stone with many arches dominated the scene and looked down upon smaller buildings of less pretension, some white, some of the same brick red, some a sandy yellow.

They had arrived.

They went straight to the large red house, the young Gurkha officer moving with the assurance that indicated he had been here many times before, knew and was known to the inhabitants, and was expected. A pair of strapping guards in tan Indian uniforms flanked the entrance. Tan turbans surmounted scowling bearded faces, and David noticed the stout "kukris", the dagger-like short native knives, tucked into their belts. They saluted the young Gurkha officer and spoke to him. He acknowledged their salute and then motioned David to follow him. The two "boys" had now dropped back to one side with their packs, settled to wait patiently until they were wanted again.

Preceded by the young Gurkha officer, David mounted the steps, crossed the wide covered porch, and went toward the door. Huge rattan sun baffles were held back to either side of the doorway, and a servant in white bowed low before them as they entered. Another servant inside bowed and gestured that they were to follow him, and they went down the long, darkly cool hall. The metal clips in his heels made David's shoes click loudly on the glasslike surface of the marble flooring, and he tried to lift his weight to soften the shattering sound. The servant, barefoot, padded silently before him. The young Gurkha officer walked beside him with a strong, loud, rhythmic tapping of his heels.

The servant paused before a tall, wide doorway. Heavy silk hangings were caught back on each side by elegant brass crooks. From behind them, almost as if on signal, another servant appeared. He spoke quietly to the first and then bowed and motioned to the young Gurkha officer and to David to follow him. The first servant bowed low again and went back to his post at the front door.

They stepped into the room. As they entered, two young men in uniform glided along one side of the room making deferential bows, nods, and gestures of recognition, and went out of the doorway through which David and the officer had just entered.

At the far end of the room, standing near a high-arched window looking out over the gardens below, stood a lone figure. He wore a turban of silk interwoven with threads of gold. His coat, cut long, tight-waisted, was buttoned to a small, straight collar. His legs were encased in tight-fitting jodhpurs. He wore no shoes. He seemed lost in his view, unaware of his guests, and then, as they were halfway across the room, he turned and came toward them.

To the young Gurkha officer he made the Indian gesture of greeting, palms together, fingers pointing upward, head slightly inclined over them. Then, as the young officer acknowledged the greeting and introduced David, he held out his hand, smiled, and spoke a perfect English "Good afternoon".

He was exotically handsome, the Gurkha chieftain. He was tall, lean, and sinewy. His skin was the colour of polished walnut. The eyes were the colour of black coffee, and there was a straight, fine-cut, aristocratic nose with small, up-cut nostrils of elegant proportion. He wore a full beard, silken black, well trimmed and gleaming as if it had been oiled. It heightened the whiteness of his teeth when he spoke and smiled.

He was disarmingly attentive to David, telling him that he knew few Americans. He asked how he liked India, how long he had been in the country, whether he had known it before the war. He indicated chairs for them to take, positioning the one for David so that he had the magnificent view from the great arched window, and then, with the attentiveness of the perfect host, he suggested that tea should be brought. It was all done with the easy friendliness of the Westerner, and it had all of the polish and manner of the perfect English gentleman.

Not a mention was made of the purpose of David's visit, not that afternoon. The purely social, casual atmosphere of an English country weekend prevailed. It was not contrived, seemingly not planned and purposeful. It was the supreme compliment of host to guest—delight in companionship, good conversation, and refreshment.

David and the young Gurkha officer were quartered in another of the houses near the main house, and each was given his own sitting-room, dressing-room and bedroom. The sanitary arrangements were primitive. The small dressing-room was provided with the bowls of scented water for the cleansing of oneself, and there were the attentions of many servants besides that of their own boys.

Dinner was of many courses, exotic, lavishly served, and highly seasoned. And it was taken alone. Servants brought a low table into David's sitting-room, placed it before a huge cushion on which he was to sit, and served him each course with meticulous courtesy. He learned later that the young Gurkha officer was served the same meal in the same fashion in his own sitting-room, and that they had eaten each course simultaneously with their host, who remained and was served in his own large house.

At the end of the meal, coffee and liqueurs were brought and placed on a low table before a huge divan. The windows were open to the soft night air, and the breeze twisted the small black-smoking flames of the low torches set about the room. A young gloriously tawny coloured girl came into the room. She wore a sari of flowing silk, her hair was drawn sleek-black tight against her head, and there was a caste mark on her forehead. She carried a long-necked, small-bodied stringed instrument.

She curtseyed low before David, smiled, and then placed a single white blossom on the table before him. With a lithe grace she moved to one side of the room, sank to her knees against a cushion, and began to stroke the strange instrument and to sing. Her voice was soft, throaty, vibrantly warm and smooth and though David could not understand a word of the songs, they were obviously of love, its trials, its longings, joys, and sadness, all expressed in tone, a look of the black eyes, a droop of the head.

David sipped his coffee, drank a brandy, and listened to the plaintive, haunting, hungering music. The girl, the voice, the strings, there was a combination of artless pleasure, a knowing innocence about them such as he had never experienced. It was like a narcotic, and he lay back against the soft cushions of the divan and closed his eyes, absorbing the wonderful sensuous sounds, seeing the fragile grace of the girl, the rich colours of the room behind his lids.

How long this went on he couldn't remember. He could only recall that he had the wonderful feeling of being out of the world, living a dream and wishing for it to go on and on forever.

The spell was broken when a servant pattered in to offer fresh coffee, more liqueurs. He had hardly left when another servant came in, bowed low, and asked if he would care perhaps for something else. Perhaps a girl? Or two? Or something more? And before David could reply, with a sweeping gesture a young girl was beckoned into the room before him. She glided past, young, prettily dark, unspoiled-looking, with firm breasts under the shimmering silk of her sari, and she was silently followed by another and another and another until six elegant, glowingly bronzed young girls had come before him, bowed low, smiled, and gone out. Some were very young, some mature, but they were all presented with Oriental enticement, the awareness that excitement lies in the unknown, not in exposure; they were groomed, sleekly draped in the most elegant of silks.

Then came the boys. A couple were perhaps in their teens, two or three others in their twenties, one or two more mature. They wore slender white trousers, but were nude from the waist up, showing either the undevelopment of their bodies or the hard, muscled mahogany sheen of their chests and shoulders. Two of them wore beards, dark and glistening, and they all wore skilfully twisted turbans of coloured silk. They bowed low before David, smiled, and glided silently from the room on bare feet.

The haunting voice and the plaintive instrument to the side of the room continued their sensuous music. The smiling servant reappeared and waited for orders.

David thanked him for his kindness, complimented him on the beauty of the young girls, the fine physiques of the young men. It was very kind of the Gurkha chieftain to provide for his pleasure, and he was grateful. But, he explained, the journey had been long, it had been tiring. He thought perhaps he would just stroll for a few minutes in the garden and then retire. He would appreciate it, however, if the singer could be instructed to continue with her music while he walked and until he was asleep.

The order was given, and the young girl smiled her pleasure.

David strolled in the garden. The night was clear and balmy, and every now and then a slight breeze would waft the delicious scent of some hidden flower. The warm, mellow voice of the girl and the subdued wail of the strings followed him as he walked, now ebbing and flowing, sometimes almost unheard and then swelling again, full and suggestive of longing, of desire, of sensual pleasure. And yet at the same time an all-consuming ennui, an enervating lassitude overcame him. It was more deadening than sleep, and he walked slowly back to his rooms in a swooning daze.

He went past the rooms of the young Gurkha officer. Soft lights shone through the gossamer silk of the hangings, and there were murmured voices, light, playful laughter, the sounds of delight.

David went on into his sitting-room. The young girl was still singing her soft melodies, strumming the strange strings and smiling. David went over to her, thanked her in English, complimented her voice and smiled. She smiled back at him and bowed her head, her slender fingers all the while playing over the strings, seducing sound from them. David said his good night to her.

He readied himself for bed, the soft singing now strangely lulling in its effect. He put out the candles and the low torches, one by one, until the room had clouded into darkness and, by contrast, the large window to the garden glowed with a silvery blue against the black of the interior. He stood for a moment in the window, breathing in the soft damp of the night, listening to the music from the next room, the laughter and the voices from the young Gurkha officer's quarters.

He was in a semi-trance with the unreality of it all when he turned back into the room. And as he sank wearily into the silken softness of the huge bed he heard, now far off, the bright laughter, the mixed voices, the mellow keening voice of the young girl, the shy whisper of the strings. . . .

The next morning David learned from the young Gurkha officer that he had passed a most pleasant evening. He had chosen three girls and one man. David never discovered how they had managed that. He was too embarrassed to ask.

It was mid-morning when David and the young Gurkha officer met with the chieftain to discuss the possibility of obtaining Gurkha fighters for OSS sabotage groups. The burden of the whole conference was on David. It was made the more pointed by the stolid listening attitude of his host. Every pause for breath, for emphasis, for a possible question, brought only a questing silence.

David explained in barest outline the objectives of the OSS against the Japanese. He explained the difficulty faced by an American organization operating in the Orient, the impossibility of using American personnel in critical areas, the hopelessness of infiltrating Americans into strategic locations with any success.

The Gurkha chieftain listened impassively.

David went on to explain what he wished to accomplish

with the Gurkha recruits. He described how our training areas would be established, how the men would be taught the latest and most refined and deadly of sabotage techniques, how they would be equipped and dispatched.

The Gurkha chieftain made no comment.

There was a long, rather awkward silence. David fought a rising inner panic. He described how the British services were cooperating with the OSS in the whole effort. He emphasized how the British had made available to us much of their training know-how, how we could utilize some of their training schools, and how, in some cases, they would be able and willing to provide instructing personnel.

The Gurkha chieftain broke his silence. He began with a long, rather scholarly and articulate summary of the history of Gurkha–British relations. His black eyes were fired with pride as he recounted the far-away exploits of the hardy Gurkha warriors. Their fierce courage, their unwavering, sure loyalty, their endurance, these he ticked off not as something to him unusual, they were routine, part of the make-up, and only to be expected of the Gurkha. He had himself served under the British in the field, and he knew first hand what such a service was like. He was bitter. And as David listened unbelieving and aghast, he poured out his hatred of the British. (WHAT LIES)

Service under the British, he went on, was dominated by condescension. No matter how highly placed a Gurkha might be in his own hierarchy, the lowliest Britisher looked down upon him. The British were stupid enough to think that they cleverly concealed their patronizing attitude but, said the Gurkha chieftain, they fooled only themselves. With an incredibly insular assurance of their own God-given superiority, they were overbearing and domineering. He sneered that the average Englishman conferred his "Good morning" on all others as if he were establishing some priceless boon. And the Englishman's manner indicated that the mere fact of his presence, his greeting, his smile, conferred some special honour on all those inferiors present.

It was all said with quiet dignity. There was no ranting, there was no heated anger; it was all expounded in an analytical, dispassionate summation. But it brought David up short with its conclusion. There would be absolutely no Gurkha assistance, no participation—at least on the part of the chieftain—in any project in which the British had the slightest influence.

Then his Oriental good manners came to the fore. He told David that he admired the Americans. He sensed that they were kind, generous, and easy to work with, though he found them vastly unworldly and naïve. On a personal level, he added that he found David a charming guest, intelligent, sincere, and amusing. He hoped he would at least stay the night and leave fresh the next morning for his return to New Delhi.

The conference was at an end.

With the guidance and counsel of the young Gurkha officer David decided to stay on the night and to use the time before his departure to think out his next moves. All that afternoon he probed his own mind, recalled the chieftain's comments, and tried to bring some success out of his mission. He had felt the sincerity of the chieftain's assessment of the Americans and the personal rapport he had established. This in itself was a gain, and if properly handled, could perhaps be exploited.

By teatime he had decided that he must go it alone, that any OSS sabotage units to be organized with Gurkha personnel would be done entirely as an American operation, without the assistance of the British. He was fully aware that he was heading into deep water, that he was putting himself in the middle between the British on the one hand and the Gurkha chieftain on the other. He was ready to risk that, to risk all of the headaches, the diplomatic niceties and double-talk to get his groups into operation.

He suggested to the young Gurkha officer that they discuss the matter further at tea with the chieftain. The idea was vetoed. It would be a breach of etiquette to discuss serious problems during the relaxing hour over tea. Another morning conference could perhaps be arranged. In this far-off nirvana it was as if the whole progress of the war could wait until the niceties of protocol had been observed, but there was nothing David could do but wait it out. After all, when the situation was viewed in proper perspective, the Gurkha chieftain was not involved in any war with the Japanese or the Nazis. Why should he feel any pressure?

They stayed that night. And the next morning, soon after breakfast, David met again with the Gurkha chieftain to assure him that it might be possible to organize a purely American effort without British assistance. He would need time—it would involve certain clearances with his superiors—but would the chieftain be willing to discuss the matter further, if such details could be worked out?

The reply was cunningly evasive. They could talk further. David would be welcome at any time he might choose to return.

They left immediately after the conference. Walking side by side, followed by their boys with the packs, David and the young Gurkha officer began the long trek back to New Delhi. But his utter discouragement of yesterday morning had vanished. There was hope that he might yet get assistance from the Gurkha chieftain.

And there had been a lusciously nubile girl with deep-black eyes, soft body, and caressing laughter.

Back in New Delhi, David used the strongest weapon of diplomacy in his dealing with the British—utter frankness. And, as might have been expected, the British reacted with a realistic, sophisticated, and practical attitude. They would keep hands off of any group of Gurkhas David could organize. In the background they stood ready to help, but the chieftain need not know that. But as for furnishing instructors, training facilities, or equipment, they would stand back. After all, it was still possible to pass on techniques, training tips, and the like to American personnel, and they in turn could do the actual handling, training, and equipping of the Gurkhas. This would salve the Gurkha pride. It would also gain the vitally important objective of getting necessary sabotage groups into the field.

David made two more tedious treks to the Gurkha chieftain's secluded stronghold. Two more times the wild contradictions of India were played out, the teeming, seething mass of aimless, starving, filthy humanity living like animals on the one hand. The quiet, the elegant luxury, the peaceful patterned indulgence of wealth and power on the other.

It had dragged on and David had returned from the latest conference discouraged. The Gurkha chieftain had been kind, he had been the perfect host, and he had been friendly, but he was still not showing his hand. There had been only one ray of light. He had assured David, at this last conference, that he would make a decision within a few days. They seemed like weeks.

Then the message arrived. It came, as did most such communications in India, by runner, another overworked "boy" who had carried the note on foot all the way from the rugged remoteness of Nepal. David could hardly wait to read it, and he was so excited at what he read in the early part of the message he hardly bothered to finish the rest. It said, in effect, that the Gurkha chieftain would be willing to cooperate with David and the OSS. He would be willing to furnish men to be trained as saboteurs. There would be one condition, however, and this was the part that David had skimmed over so lightly in his excitement. The Gurkha chieftain would furnish the required recruits if David would act as sponsor for the Gurkha chieftain's daughter.

David read that part of the letter over a couple of times. It seemed reasonable enough—no problem. It was not until the young Gurkha officer had explained to him what such a sponsorship meant that David realized the complexities of the negotiations in which he was involved.

To sponsor the Gurkha chieftain's daughter was the highest honour he could bestow upon David, it was explained. It was in this manner that the Gurkha chieftain was pledging his word, sealing his bond, and guaranteeing his good faith. Its acceptance by David would be equally binding on him as an act of the highest faith, akin only to writing one's pledge in one's own blood. To refuse to act as sponsor was unthinkable. The honour was not given lightly. It was bestowed only on those persons singled out for social favour, and bestowed only after much careful thought. To refuse could only be interpreted as an insult, an insult of the most damning and shaming kind.

All of this was explained carefully to David. And the tone of the young Gurkha officer's voice indicated the reverence with which he regarded this honour.

David listened to it all and then asked what his responsibilities as a sponsor would be. He wondered to himself if he might be assuming some obligation for the girl's upbringing, her future welfare or education.

The young Gurkha officer explained it all quite simply. As sponsor, David would be expected to break the young lady's virginity.

There was no turning back.

As the young Gurkha officer had explained, the offer of a

sponsorship was such a high honour there could only be an acceptance. It was the highest pledge of fealty, other than his very life, that a Gurkha could provide. It meant eternal loyalty and friendship. To refuse such a proffer would be unthinkable and would incur Gurkha enmity and hatred to the death. So, by messenger, the word went back that the young American officer would be most honoured to act as sponsor for the Gurkha chieftain's daughter.

There were more messages, back and forth. They were all highly stylized and formal. They expressed the Gurkha chieftain's delight. They thanked the young American officer for the high honour he was conferring on them all. They set the date. It was also suggested that David should plan to arrive at least a day and preferably two days in advance of the "ceremony".

In the company of the young Gurkha officer, on whom he now leaned more heavily than ever for advice, David arrived at the Gurkha chieftain's headquarters. The Gurkha chieftain came forward to meet him in the hallway of the huge redstone house, effusive in his greeting. He was most solicitous for David's comfort, and he accompanied him to his quarters. They were in a different house this time, larger and more richly appointed than the one he had been assigned before, and as soon as he was left to himself David found the servants about him lavish in their deference, vying with each other to wait on him. It was, as he explained it later, like living an unbelievably exotic film.

Again the pageantry of the evenings was played out, and the days were spent in the idle enjoyment of the beauty of the setting. David walked the gardens, listened to the play of the small fountains, and wondered at the unrealism of the setting, the people, the situation in which he found himself. He dared not inquire about the daughter, and yet he found himself wondering about her, visualizing her. There were moments of panic when he found himself overwhelmed with embarrassment and shyness. Wide awake, he dreamed nightmares. They ran the gamut from finding himself with the ugliest of old spinsters to discovering the most beautiful of mocha-coloured bodies. He worried over the form, what would be done, how they would be introduced, and always he came back to a sweating terror of what lay before him, what was expected of him.

It was evening when they began preparing David for his sponsorship. Three servants came to his dressing-room and, bowing low, explained that they would now ready him for the ceremony. One of the servants stood aside and gave hushed commands to the two others, and they began at once to disrobe him. They removed his uniform, all of his clothes, until he was completely nude. Then, with bows and gestures, they asked him to lie on a couch over which fresh sheets had been spread. Working deftly and with meticulous care, the two servants began bathing his whole body with warm, scented water to which had been added a light sweet oil.

They complimented him on the broadness of his shoulders, the depth of his chest, the flatness of his stomach, and the trim tautness of his hips. They admired the firm muscles of his long legs, and they were delighted with his masculinity. They commented quite openly and frankly on his sexual organs as they bathed and oiled him. It was not snide, bawdy comment, but quite simply observant; they were delighted at what they saw, they said so, and they were happy for the young lady who was to have so fine a sponsor. It would have been too embarrassing to bear had it not all been done with such innocent candour.

There was a tingling sensation of well-being when at last they asked him to rise from the couch. One of the servants handed him a comb and brush and held a glass for him as he parted and combed his hair. When he had finished, they held a kimono of sheer silk for him and they helped him to tie it around his waist. It was elegantly embroidered with designs of birds and flowers in various colours and there was much heavy gold thread worked into the pattern. They slipped soft silken sandals on to his feet, held in place with toe thongs.

He was ready.

In a few moments the Gurkha chieftain appeared. He bowed to David, shook hands with him, complimented him on his appearance, and asked if he was ready. David felt a sudden wave of panic flow through his body. There was a tightening in this throat, but he managed an affirmative answer. Without any more conversation the Gurkha chieftain asked him to follow, as he led the way to the house.

Two strapping Gurkhas stood at the door. They were in dress uniform, with short curved kukris stuck into their belts, and there were coloured turbans meticulously twisted on to their heads. Full, black beards gave them a fearsome look and glistened in the soft yellow light of the torches they were carrying. The chieftain spoke to them, and the little procession moved off across the garden. The flaming torches lighted the way with a flickering golden glow and gave off a scented, oily black smoke in languid wisps.

At the far end of the garden, glowing softly yellow from the flickering torches within, was a small tent of golden silk. Seeing it now for the first time. David wondered that he had not noticed in on his walk that afternoon, and yet it fitted so well into the background and the setting of the garden that it could have been a permanent structure, rather than a tent. He was conscious of the fact that his two servants, like the slaves they were, had come quietly up behind them and were now walking with them toward the tent. A few more paces, and they were there.

Without hesitation the Gurkha chieftain stepped between the softly draped hangings of the opening. He had David by the arm and led him along with him. A deep-piled oriental carpet covered the ground, several low torches glowed silently, and there was a heavy scent of musk, heady, exotic, almost stifling. Directly opposite the entrance and perhaps four feet in front of them, there was a wide, low couch. It was raised only a few inches above the carpet level, as if someone had simply lain a mattress on the ground, but it was covered with shimmering sheer silk of the purest white. There were many pillows covered in the same white silk scattered about the head of the couch.

Two handsome women in silken saris were in the tent and they bowed low, their heads almost touching the ground, when the chieftain entered. He spoke to them in Khas-kura, the Gorkahli dialect of Pahari, something David did not understand. The two women bowed again, backed away, and then disappeared through a curtained slit at the back of the tent.

They reappeared as silently as they had left. It seemed to David they had had time to do little more than turn around, and yet there was nothing hurried, no fluster or haste about them, only a quiet, gliding, lithe efficiency. They stopped just inside the silken room, turned, and holding back the drapery of the entrance bowed toward the opening.

The small, slight figure of a girl appeared in the curtained entry. Her head was bowed. The black hair, glistening like patent leather in the flickering light, was parted in the middle and drawn tightly back against her head into a knot on her neck. She wore a sheer sari of the palest yellow silk, so pale it looked almost white against the rich tan colour of her skin, the black of her hair. Her hands were clasped in front of her. She was barefoot.

The two women urged her forward until she was directly in front of the Gurkha chieftain and David. She stopped when she was about a yard from them, bowed low, and then went to her knees and prostrated herself before them on the carpet. The Gurkha chieftain spoke swiftly to her in Khas-kura. The words meant nothing to David, but he understood the warmth of the tone, the kindly, compassionate manner. Then, in English, he asked the girl to rise and introduced her to David.

Gracefully, with the sinuous muscle-tensing of a cat, she rose from the ground and slowly raised her head. And for the first time David looked into her eyes. They were the wide, darkly wondering, and frightened eyes of a child.

David almost blurted his shock aloud. Only the whole dreamlike sequence of what he was experiencing kept him from some violent reaction. He only stared in disbelief. Nothing that was being said now meant anything to him. His brain was a wild turmoil of emotions. At no time, not once in all of the weeks and days of preparation for this occasion, had he for a moment suspected or expected that the daughter whom he would be sponsoring would be a child. A child of twelve, at the most, and perhaps only of eleven or even ten, who could tell?

Frantically, within himself, David fought a wild impulse to run. Everything in his background rebelled against what was before him, and he was overcome with an inner revulsion. Yet there was no escape. He head reeled in a confused, turbulent jumble of thought and emotion. It all added up to panic, a panic so overwhelming as to immobilize him completely.

Beside him he heard the Gurkha chieftain speaking. Whether it was to him or to the girl he didn't know. They were only words, heard but unregistered. He stood transfixed, stunned, weakened with a strange kind of terror.

Somewhere in the background, outside the tent, there was music, the plaintive wail of strings, the longing throb of a voice.

The two older women came forward, took the child by the hand, and led her to the couch. Deftly, gently, they undid the knot of her hair until it fell in a glistening coil down her back.

One of the women brushed it with a silver-backed brush until it lay soft over her shoulders. Then they unwrapped the silken folds of her sari. They spoke softly to her, and she lay down on the shimmering whiteness of the sheets. The women drew back the sari until it was quite free of her body and she was momentarily exposed. Then, artfully, they arranged the filmy material loosely across her tiny body. They placed pillows under her head, patted them, and smoothed the sheets. Then, quietly, they turned, bowed, smiled at the Gurkha chieftain and at David, and withdrew from the tent.

The Gurkha chieftain smiled at David, nodded, and gestured toward the couch where the child lay. Then, as David stood motionless, he took him gently by the arm and walked him to the edge of the couch. He smiled again, bowed, turned abruptly and left the scented silken room.

David stood and looked down at the child. She was watching him with wide, inquiring eyes, intensely black. He was hesitant, embarrassed, and once again there was the overpowering urge to run. In the background the haunting music cajoled, urged, enticed.

He smiled at her.

She returned the smile. Then, with a completely innocent gesture, she raised both arms toward him and wriggled her fingers in invitation.

"You lie here? Please?"

It was half question, half invitation, and it was spoken with studied schoolgirl precision. Her voice was small, immature. Then, in a manner that suggested hours of practice, with a studied parody of everything sensual, she squirmed her small body in the softness of the couch and drew the sari partly away from her breasts. They were pathetically small, only just beginning to show any budding form, an emphasis to her immaturity.

David slid on to the couch. There was no desire in him at all, only an all-encompassing impotence. He felt weakened, helplessly spent, and he lay quietly beside the tiny dark child, as uninvolved as if she had been a doll.

It suddenly occurred to him that he didn't even know her name. He turned to her and asked it.

"Lahni."

Again the precise child's voice. The large, dark, fearful, and wondering eyes burned into him.

135

He asked about her life, what she liked to do, whether or not she had brothers and sisters. It was a frantic effort to avoid what was expected of him.

She was polite. She answered him slowly, carefully, pronouncing all of her words with great precision. They were only answers. She made no effort at conversation, no effort to keep the talk going. Then, when there was a sudden lag, she drew herself closer to him until their bodies touched and her head was resting in the crook of his shoulder.

"Not talk. We love."

The dark child-eyes looked into his fixedly. She had freed herself completely from her sari and her lean, small body, the colour of ginger against the whiteness of the sheets, pressed against him seductively.

Still David resisted. He felt nothing of passion, and he lay inert, hopelessly incapable of performing his proper function.

The two older women apparently had done their work well. The girl-child caressed him with the studied intensity of the most seductive courtesan. She slipped her hands under his kimono, rippled her fingers across his chest, stroked his arms and shoulders. She nestled against him with little murmuring sounds of contentment while the eager, lightly avid hands and fingers played along his back, around his waist, and over the curve of his buttocks with little pats of affection. They retraced their play, the arms, the shoulders, the chest again, and then wandered over the smooth flatness of his stomach.

It was all done with lightness, and yet somehow it lacked spontaneity. It was studied, too obviously rehearsed, the careful work of a beginner in the art of giving pleasure to a man. Without knowing or fully understanding or really feeling what she was doing, this tiny child was acting out what she had been taught by her more experienced tutors. It was the beginning, for her, of a life of complete submission to the male, a life to be devoted to giving pleasure, always pleasure and delight, to the dominant sex.

The fingers continued their searching play, lightly still, perhaps a trifle more urgently, along the back, the waist, the legs. Then, with a childlike impatience, she tugged petulantly at the sash that bound his kimono, undid it, and pulled the soft silk away from his body.

"You take away? Yes?"

David rolled away from her to the edge of the couch. With

his back to her, he stood quickly and slipped off the kimono. Naked, he sat back on the edge of the couch, then lay at full length and turned toward her.

She raised herself partly on one elbow and candidly looked over his body. Playfully she drew a finger along the line where his shorts had hindered his tan, and in another moment the restless fingers had found the soft warmth of his genitals. They probed tentatively, inquiringly, with a gentle caressing and then, impulsively, the girl-child drew herself closer to him, one small, warm, smooth leg thrust provocatively between his own.

The sensuous, longing, throbbing urge of the music rose and fell. The seductive voice, the plaintive strings, the mood was licentious. The soft light, the heavy scent of the musk and the incense. The insistence, the urgent play of the warm small body beside him. The male in David responded.

He took the girl-child in his arms and embraced her. There was a sudden tensing of her body, a resisting moment, a tiny, suppressed cry of quick pain, and he had penetrated her. She clung to him, she pulled at him, tore and pressed and pounded against him in a terrifying agony of sensation, until it seemed to him that the very size and weight of his body would crush her lifeless. Then, in the quickening ecstasy when it seemed as if the very world would burst around them, there was a sudden tremor, her fury was released, the climax was achieved, and they fell back exhausted.

She lay close against him, their bodies moist-warm and melded. He could feel her heart beating rapidly against him, and the deep exhaustion of her breathing warmed the base of his throat. He stroked the small soft back, cupped her firm buttocks in his hand, and caressed her arms, her shoulders, the silken blackness of her hair.

He reached for his kimono on the carpet beside him and drew it across their naked bodies. She opened her eyes, smiled up at him, then closed them again and snuggled closer, to sleep. There were large liquid pools of tears bathing the dark pupils, and they were forced down her cheeks in drops with the closing of her lids. David whisked them away lightly with a corner of the kimono, bent her head forward, and kissed her on the hair.

In the background the fluid sounds of the voice and the strings were still to be heard. David closed his eyes. It was soothing, there was a sudden wonderful release of all tension, and he slept.

The discreet small sounds of the servants woke him. They were padding quietly about on the carpeting of the tent, a polite way of urging him on to other things. He woke easily, looking up at the silken ceiling of the tent. The soft light of the flaring torches caused a shimmering of the golden folds, and in a moment it all came back to him. It was a reality, not a dream.

He turned to the girl-child.

She was gone.

A servant came forward holding another robe for him, and David rose, slipped into the robe, the slippers. With a servant either side of him carrying a torch, he went back to the guest-house. There they bathed him again with more warm scented waters and helped him to dress in his best uniform. It had been pressed and the brass had been polished until he hardly recognized it for his own.

Fully dressed, with the servants as escorts lighting the way, David was ushered to the Gurkha chieftain's large red-stone house. It was brilliantly lighted with many torches and candles, and there was a dinner party laid out in David's honour.

The Gurkha chieftain was in his most expansive mood. He was elegantly dressed in a costume of heavily embroidered silk, there was much gold lacing in his turban, and the curved kukri at his waist was encased in a jewelled scabbard. The young Gurkha officer was there, and there were some six or eight other officers. There were no women, not as guests. But there was a lavish feast, there was music, and there were dancing girls. And there were toasts drunk: to David, to the Gurkha chieftain, to the Americans, to Gurkha–American friendship.

The party went on well into the night. The flickering lights, the music, the sensuous, invitational elegance of the gloriously dark girls dancing with sinuous grace, the innumerable slaves bringing ever more delights, it was exotically stimulating. The soft warmth of the night air drowsing through the high-arched windows, the heavy scent of musk and incense, it was a drugging of the senses with motion, colour, sound, scent, and suggestion as sure as any narcotic. No other world seemed to exist. And even this one seemed unreal, beyond any tangible grasp, the hallucinations of hashish.

At last David made his way back to his quarters with the

two servants in attendance. They helped ready him for bed, they tended his every need, and they were solicitious of anything further he might wish. There was one marked omission. It must have been a matter of form, a part of the intricate etiquette of this ritualistic world. For the first time in any of his visits to the Gurkha chieftain, David was not offered his choice of sexual diversion.

From the young Gurkha officer he learned the next morning that all of the other guests continued the night's revelry. with private delights. It was the custom.

David's sponsorship paid off.

There was a final conference the next morning before he returned to New Delhi. All of the details were then worked out, and the Gurkha chieftain agreed to supply the necessary recruits for the OSS sabotage teams. After all, in a world where slavery was the accepted thing, there was no manpower problem, once the highest authority had agreed to one's terms. The chieftain's earlier crafty reticence had vanished, and he came to treat David almost as a son; there was nothing he would not do for the young American.

A seemingly endless stream of raw material in the form of young Gurkha warriors became available to David for training. They were sent to OSS schools where they were taught the intricate and devious ways of sabotage. They were given instruction in basic chemistry so that they could fashion explosives from whatever might be at hand. They were taught how to identify the most vulnerable areas of basic machinery such as locomotives, trucks, tankers, generators, planes, tanks, and the like. And then how to disable them. They were taught codes. They were instructed in parachuting and the camouflage that necessarily went with it. They were taught how to kill—silently.

The Gurkhas were apt pupils. Their tremendous daring and courage, their physical stamina, their pride, all of these factors contributed to their success in sabotage work. And when at last David was able to get them into the war areas, teams of two or three men working surreptitiously behind enemy lines, they were tremendously effective against the Japanese.

They went far beyond the primary function of the saboteur. They were so in love with the intrigue of the game, so filled with the challenge and the excitement of the tasks assigned to them, many of the Gurkhas branched out into a kind of guerrilla warfare of their own, until no Japanese persons or places could be considered safe from the deadly attacks of the OSS-trained Gurkha saboteurs.

Life meant nothing to them. And in this respect they were perhaps the only effective warriors the Allied forces put into the field who could match the death-defying insouciance of the Japanese kamikaze fighters. Such was the war-fever blood-lust of the Gurkha in action he had no regard for his own safety, only the unquenchable drive to attain his objective, whatever it might be.

All of this David accomplished through the sponsorship of the Gurkha chieftain's daughter. Weeks of preparation and parley, months of training, and then the added months of the most desperate and dangerous kind of warfare—all of this hinged on the single bizarre factor, the deflowering of one small girl in the remote garden in Nepal.

One young American, born and bred, indoctrinated in the solid virtues of mid-country America, challenged by the unfamiliar ritual of an ancient society in the form of one small girl-child.

And he never saw her again.

The war was long over. Fifteen, perhaps eighteen, years had passed since the Japanese surrender. It was all now history, something one never seemed to think of any more, like a bad dream buried. I was crossing the Atlantic on the *Queen Mary*. She was peculiarly special to me, the *Mary*, because in her wartime grey paint, as troopship, she had brought me back home after it was all over. It gave her a slight edge on the *Queen Elizabeth*, which had taken me into the whole mess in 1942.

It was the second night out from New York, and I was quietly reading in the lounge. Since it was a late autumn crossing, there were few passengers in first class, and I looked up as someone came toward me across the room.

It was David.

He was bronzed, still lean and young-looking though there were a few grey hairs showing at the temples. He was, of course, in civilian clothes. I had not the slightest idea where he had been living, what he was doing, what his life had been since the war, and suddenly he was there. The chance of the meeting, the unexpectedness of it, the years of life to be covered, the experiences to be relived and exchanged, it all made for the fastest crossing of the Atlantic I ever made, jet planes included.

We got all of the personals out of the way at once. I learned that David was now in business for himself, that he was successful beyond his wildest hopes, and that his work took him abroad at least once a year and often more. It was a happy story.

But what was infinitely more important to both of us was the sudden going back in time. All at once, here was the rare chance to relive those incredible days in the OSS. This is something no outsider can understand. It stems basically from the fact that so much of one's life in the OSS was tinged with the unusual, the slightly mad, the always strange and unbelievable. To talk of these things with someone who had not been in the organization is impossible. The outsider would only look at one as slightly deranged, or at best a weaver of tall tales. The fellow graduate, the former OSS man, he understands. He knows these things and more did happen.

We exchanged information on who was where, doing what, and all the rest. We swapped yarns about the General, the wonderful "Wild Bill" Donovan who had headed the OSS, had beeen close to us both, the man known to every person in the OSS as 109, his code number.

And we talked about India, Nepal, Assam, the Gurkha sabotage groups, and the sponsorship. David had the wonderful gift of seeing himself clearly, and we laughed over the embarrassment he encountered in his dealing with the Gurkhas. He laughed about how naïve and unsophisticated he had been when he was first thrown into the intrigues of India, and as he described his ordeal leading up to the sponsorship and all that it involved, he embellished the tale with little asides. He pictured himself as the shy country bumpkin. He painted himself as sex-shy, embarrassed, and inept. And he laughed over what "the folks back home" would have said of his shenanigans.

I couldn't resist interjecting my own surmise as to what some wool-hat member of Congress or the Senate would do with the tale of a young red-blooded American boy being sent to war to seduce young virgins. With government money, too. Unvouchered funds, the secret currencies I had been charged with dispensing for the furtherance of the clandestine activities of the OSS. The prospect of Congressional reaction to all this made for some amusing visions.

The unreality of the whole thing struck us again. It had seemed unreal to David even as it happened, and now, reliving it in the lounge of the *Queen Mary* at sea, years later, the dream sequence was even stronger. And we both agreed that it was the kind of life that one kept to oneself, or shared only with the few initiated, the former OSS people. No one else would understand.

We became philosophical and serious after all the laughter and the amusement.

David took a drink from the tall glass in front of him and fingered the frosted moisture on the outside of the glass. The smile-marks that always creased his cheeks each side of his mouth, when he was amused, vanished and there was a wrinkling of the brow, thoughtful, serious.

"You know, Bob, it's a funny feeling. I sometimes wonder if maybe I've got a little bastard running around India somewhere. Half me, half Gurkha. . . . Crazy war."

CHAPTER FOUR

OLAF

THE night was right for it.

There was a cold, steady drizzle of rain, and every now and then a gale-like whip of wind from off the Norwegian Sea gave the drops the cutting force of small ice daggers. Along the Bergen waterfront it was black-dark in the wartime blackout, and the wet shine of the rain on the cobbles made it almost impossible to tell where the city ended and the sea began. Only the hooded dull-yellow glow of a few essential street lights, a police post, a quay light, a ship light, the occasional bobbing yellow disk of a pedestrian flashlight on the pavement, only these relieved the cold drenching gloom.

Few were out. The occupation German storm troopers had, for the most part, taken shelter. After all, they were confident in their domination of a prostrate Norway. It left the cold, rain-lashed streets to the dockers and stevedores, the seamen, the fishermen, the odd German soldier looking for a drink, a girl, a bit of *fisk*, or a warm, glowing place for a few moments of relaxation and talk. Other than these the port of Bergen, the second city of Norway and one of its important ports, was as deserted as a country town at midnight.

Olaf had spotted him first.

He was seated at the end of the bar in the little waterfront café, ignored by the rest of the customers. He was obviously alone, occupied only by his drink in its tall glass, and he was wearing the uniform and insignia of a lieutenant in the German occupation army. He was tall and lean and blond, and the thing that was important to Olaf was that he was very like himself in his physical characteristics.

Olaf spoke to the two men with him and, quietly so that there would be no sudden turning on the part of anyone, asked what they thought. Was this the one? Could this be their chance?

One of the men rose from their table and walked up to the bar. He moved casually, came close to the young German lieutenant, and reached for a toothpick on the bar. He spilled a few, cursed his clumsiness, and as he picked them up and placed them back in the little glass cup, he studied the face of the young German nearby. The face, the line of the nose and the cheeks, the eyes. He finished with the toothpicks, turned, and went back to the table with Olaf and his other companion.

"As close as you'll ever get. If you still want to go through with it."

"Does he look like me? What about the eyes, the teeth? They're always the give-away." Olaf suppressed his excitement. "What about them?"

"He's got your baby-blue eyes," teased his companion. "I didn't ask him to show me his teeth."

Olaf was silent. He was thinking and he was studying the young German as he ran his fingers up and down the cool moisture of his glass. His two companions went on with their drinking, all the while continuing their appraisal of the young German lieutenant at the end of the bar. A kind of foreboding quiet encased them like a caul.

They sat this way in silence, the three men, drinking slowly and smoking for perhaps another ten minutes. And yet, with no further words passing between them, with no further discussion of the matter at hand, they had reached agreement. The decision had been made. Silently, by some kind of inner telepathy they knew, all three of them, that this was it.

The young German paid for his drink, slid from the bar stool, and turned to go. He stood surveying the dim, smoke-shrouded room with a kind of arrogance while he buttoned the long, heavy grey field overcoat about him against the weather. Then, when he was quite ready, he picked up his gloves, pulled them on, and strode from the room. A sudden silence filled the café as he walked to the door, and it seemed as if every eye in the small room was hatefully on him as he strode unseeing between the small tables.

Olaf, with the others, watched him go. Then, as the German reached the door, Olaf rose. He did it casually. He took his coat and put it on, he drew a scarf about his neck, and he buttoned his coat as he stood by the table. His every motion was deliberate, unhurried, easy, in direct contrast to the urgency and excitement that were beginning to rise within him. He counted out the money for their drinks, placed it on the table, and waved to the bartender to indicate that the payment was there. With his two companions he left the café.

Almost without looking, Olaf knew the direction the young German lieutenant would take. The Germans had taken over a large building near the centre of the city for the billeting of their occupational troops, officers and men in the same large area, and it would be there that the lieutenant would be heading.

He must have waited a minute or two on the steps of the café when he went out, the German lieutenant, because he was just a short distance away when Olaf went into the street. In the black murk, in the bite and slash of the icy rain, Olaf could hear the arrogant thrust of his boots against the cobbles, and he could see the bright platter of light just before his feet as he walked. The Germans always carried stronger flashlights than the natives.

In an instant Olaf abandoned his studied nonchalance. With a sign to his two companions to move quickly and quietly, he raised himself to his tiptoes and hurried over the pavement in pursuit of the German. Olaf knew the area well. Through a marketplace, then along an important street, a small square, then a turn into a side street of small shops. They would be closed and shuttered late at night, dark, darker than ever in the wild howl of the rain and the wind. That would be it.

Olaf and his two companions stalked their quarry. The forceful stride of the German kept them alert to his whereabouts, and the bright silvery-white lozenge of light that wavered and danced in front of his feet, just a glow beyond the limits of his stride, gave them a perfect visual clue as to every move and turn.

They met no one. They saw or heard no other moving thing in the tense tracking, the chill shadowing of their victim. They were alone, four men in a morass of dark.

The German crossed the little square at the diagonal. His head was drawn down into his collar, bent against the cut of the wind and the rain, and he was hurrying now to get in from the fierce flooding cut and slash of the elements. Across the square he turned into the side street and headed for his billet. Another two blocks, and he would be there.

Olaf closed the gap, his two companions close behind him. They were moving close to the building, now single file, walking lightly on tiptoe, tensed and ready. The blue-white circle of light bounced ahead of them only a couple of paces. In the narrow funnel of the street, the gusty rain howled almost horizontally against them, and there was a high-pitched whine that extinguished all other sound.

Olaf raised his hand in signal to his two companions. Then, with the tiptoe stealth and grace of a leopard on kill, he lurched toward the bent figure of the young German lieutenant in front of him. He was almost off the ground when he struck, and at the very instant of body contact he had cast his garrotte over the head of the unsuspecting German. With practised skill he tightened the garotte even as the figure lunged forward to the pavement. Something shot past him at the same moment, there was a sickening dull thud of metal against flesh and bone as one of his companions caught the German on the skull with a spring cosh, and in another moment Olaf was kneeling on the back of the inert German on the greasy wetness of the pavement.

There had not been a grunt, not a sigh, not a sign of any kind, to indicate that the German ever knew what hit him.

Quickly Olaf and his two accomplices dragged the body into the arcade of a small shop. They worked now with the precision of a team that had planned well in advance every detail of their mission. Without more than a nod one of the accomplices moved quickly away and disappeared in the howling murk and the wet. Olaf and his other helper were already beginning to undress the dead German, and in a matter of moments they had him stripped to his bare skin. Not a motion was wasted. While the last few items were being removed from the German, Olaf began to undress himself. Not daring to risk less, in case of capture and the inevitable bare-skin examination that would follow, he stripped naked and, wet and shivering, quickly pulled on the dead German's underwear. Shirt, trousers, tunic, boots, they all fitted him passably well, at least well enough for his purpose. With his own discarded shirt he cleaned the wet dirt as best he could from the heavy field overcoat with the German insignia, and he was only beginning to button it when his second companion reappeared. He was carrying a small parcel and a bottle.

Olaf congratulated him on the speed with which he had completed his errand. Then, fully dressed in the uniform, the greatcoat, and the military cap of the young German lieutenant, Olaf stood for the approval of his two companions. One of them played a flashlight up and down his figure, toe to head, head to toe. The success of the impersonation was obvious from the impulsive astonishment with which they examined him.

Olaf searched the pockets of the uniform, found the wallet, the officer's identity card, his name, serial number, and related essentials. He repeated the German name over to himself a couple of times to make it stick. He spoke a few words of sharp, harsh German, and he couldn't resist a mock "Heil Hitler" with a flat-handed salute. He was ready.

He picked up the parcel that his companion had brought. He tucked the bottle carefully under his arm. And without as much as a glance at the nude body sprawled at his feet, he stepped into the street. He continued in the direction the German officer had been heading. The billet would be less than two blocks away. Fortunately it was a building that Olaf had known slightly prior to the Nazi occupation, and although he had not been inside it since it had been taken over by the Germans, he approached it with the confidence of one who knew exactly where he was going.

There was a dull pinpoint of light either side of the door to the building, and the water was pouring down the façade in an inky film as he cast his flashlight quickly over the stonework. He had his papers ready in the side pocket of the greatcoat, anxious that there be not too much delay, too much time at whatever checkpoint he might encounter inside. There was a tension in his body now, a kind of tingling excitement, and it seemed to mount with each step as he climbed them firmly and pushed open the door.

A sudden brightness made him squint, and he turned against it as he closed the door quickly behind him. He stood for a moment, loosened his greatcoat and shook the sodden surplus of rain from it before he went any farther. He was in a small vestibule glassed away from the main hall and he could look in to what lay ahead without yet seeming to be a part of it.

A young heavy-set officer, a sergeant, was seated behind a desk. He was reading, and it appeared that he had not heard Olaf enter the vestibule. At least he took no notice of him until he opened the glass doors and went into the hall. Then, with the reflex action of a puppet, the young sergeant stood at attention, gave the Nazi salute, snapped "Heil Hitler", and pushed the sign-in register toward Olaf. He hardly looked at him.

Olaf took the pen that was hitched to the book with a beaded chain, signed the German lieutenant's name with a squiggle, and turned away. As he did so he spoke in German to the duty officer and told him that he would be going out again in a short while. Special duty. Most of the night. And what a night. He was almost out of hearing as the young sergeant commiserated with him.

The stairwell was to one side of the main hall, and Olaf walked to it with a firm stride. There was no one, no one about in the halls, on the stairs, only the duty officer back at his desk. Olaf stood by the stairwell for a moment and listened. Silence.

Quickly he went down the stairs to the basement. There was a door at the bottom of the stairs, and he opened it cautiously. A couple of dim emergency lights glowed in the cavernous gloom, coal-grimed and dusty, and he stood again to listen. And when there was no sound he moved on toward the huge furnace that grumbled warmly in the dark. A rat scuttled into the shadows and startled him. Carefully he put down the parcel and the bottle and took off his greatcoat. Freed of its sodden weight, he suddenly felt alert and without delay he set to his task. He unwrapped the parcel. It was carefully done up, and he silently thanked his accomplice for the waterproof casing that now served up to him completely dry and function-ready explosives.

With a deft sureness of touch that had come from long practice, practice under stress, Olaf set his charge. He found the most vulnerable spot, placed the charge, secured the fuse, set the timer. He checked it out a couple of times to be sure; then, against the possibility he might meet someone upstairs, he carefully re-wrapped his parcel, held it and the bottle under the greatcoat over his arm, and went back up the stairs.

At the second-floor level he sought out the latrine. Corridor lights, lights in the latrine, all of this helped, and he was able to set another charge, fuse it, and time-set it to follow the boiler room by a few seconds. The heavy sleeping sounds of the men in the barracks rooms acted as a kind of soothing encouragement to him as he worked.

He went the length of the corridor on the second floor, went down a rear stairwell to the first, and just for good measure set a third charge in the heavy stonework of the stairwell. This he set to follow the second charge by a matter of seconds.

He was whistling softly to himself as he walked the ground floor hall and approached the duty officer's desk. The same young servant was there, still poring over his books, and he rose again like a puppet—attention, "Heil Hitler", and the staccato salute. He pushed the book toward Olaf and then looked at his watch. The big clock behind his desk said it was twenty minutes past one in the morning.

Olaf signed the book again, put in the time, and placed the pen back in its holder. He made a mental note of the fact that he had been in the building about half an hour. Then, quite impulsively, he took the bottle from under his arm and handed it to the sergeant. He explained that he wouldn't have time for it himself. Perhaps the sergeant would like it. Did he like Norwegian beer?

The bottle had served its purpose. It was a simple decoy to distract attention from the parcel of fuses, timers, and explosives he had brought in with him.

Olaf buttoned the greatcoat high around his neck and made ready to face the cold wet of the night. He walked slowly away from the guard's desk, casually buttoning the coat as he went. The young sergeant had already opened the bottle and taken a healthy swig from it and was back at the paperwork on the desk before him. Olaf pushed open the glass doors of the vestibule, then the heavier outer doors, and he was on the steps.

The storm was still raging. Wind, driving rain, low cloud—it was ugly weather, but it had served its purpose. Olaf saw not one moving creature on his way back to the little house where he and his two accomplices had a room.

They were waiting for him. Thoughtfully, they had built up the coal fire in the grate so that the room was glowingly warm, and they had some bread, cheese, and strong drink ready. Olaf stripped off the dead German's clothes and wrapped himself in a wool robe, and while they ate and drank by the fire they compared notes.

Olaf told them about his work, how easy it had been, easier than he had thought possible, and he suggested that all the German clothing be kept. It just might come in handy for some other job. His two accomplices told him how they had disposed of the body. Wrapped in an oilskin, hoisted to their shoulders like a log, they had carried the dead German to the harbour, weighted the body with cobbles lashed into the wrapping, and dumped him into the water. It had been easy. No one had seen them, and if they had, in Norway, seething under the Nazi heel, it was doubtful if even the police would have interfered where a German was involved.

They were asleep when it happened.

And they were back at their regular jobs at the usual time the next morning. Even then there were rumours, but it wasn't until they joined the groups at the little restaurant in the evening that they heard the details. The building had been badly damaged. There had been many casualties. Dozens had been injured, and someone said that there were over thirty dead. The correct numbers were hard to come by, because the Germans were not giving out any information.

The rumours were wild. Some said the boiler had blown up. Others said it was sabotage. There had been a series of explosions. Some said ammunition stored in the building had ignited. Others said they had heard that it was a petrol storage tank that had gone up. No one knew.

Olaf listened to them in silence. Someone said that whatever it was, it was probably because some German had been stupid. Careless. They were stupid, the Germans.

Olaf said yes, they were.

Of all of the countries that came under the cruelly sadistic domination of the Nazis during World War II, Norway offered perhaps the most fanatic resistance. There was a kind of calm, cold, and calculating defiance in the Norwegian character that stood for no compromise. It was almost as if the real Norwegian patriots felt an added courage, a more intense loyalty needed display to offset the shame of Quisling, the traitor whose defection to the Nazi cause was so notorious his very name has become an accepted word for traitor.

Where the resistance in other countries, France, the Low Countries, Poland, Italy, Yugoslavia, and the like was just as strong and just as effective, there was an intensely cold hatred in the Norwegian activity that hid under impassivity. There was nothing they would not try; and whatever it was, it was done with an impersonal aura of non-involvement, accepted almost as a natural function. The person did not matter.

Olaf was typical. Yet perhaps that is not quite right. Olaf was an exceptional individual, a rare individual, but there were many like him, if in lower key. In that respect he was typical. In every other way he was an original.

In the deadly "for keeps" game of espionage and sabotage, one comes in contact with every kind of personality. OSS had them all. Intellectuals and thugs, scientists and artists. Rotarians and aesthetes, realists and dreamers—you name it, we had it. But of all these, and there were literally hundreds of every category, Olaf was the only one I ever knew who was in a class by himself. For Olaf was the nearest thing in the modern world to the professional adventurer, soldier of fortune, mercenary, choose what tag you will.

Olaf sought excitement. And the greater the danger, the more difficult the conditions of the game, the higher the stakes, the more intense became his involvement.

I'm not sure that he ever held a humdrum, run-of-the-mill job in his life. Certainly not for any length of time. But by the time he came to us, in his mid-thirties, he had been all over the world. He had been a stowaway, a regular seaman, a docker and roustabout. He had fought in the Far East in local skirmishes, he had fought in the Middle East in other disputes, and he had skied and adventured and brawled the length and breadth of Europe. Always he had left when the excitement and the danger subsided, and always he had gone back to the land he loved as no other—Norway.

He came to the OSS quite frankly because it offered him, for the first time in his life, the chance for real excitement and danger in a setting he knew from birth and fiercely loved. One might say it was the first crusade. All else had been "for kicks".

After the occupation of Norway by the Germans in 1940, Olaf made his way to England. It was in London that we recruited him.

Tall, lean, blond, blond, blond, with pale blue eyes and even, slightly sensuous features. Olaf was the cliché of the "handsome devil". And he knew it. He was a wild man with the ladies, and he went through them as one would a smorgasbord, tasting and sampling, consuming and discarding on whim. There were always more.

This was a worry and a flaw, and he was cautioned that once operational in occupied Norway, women could be treacherous. Women and money. And I can remember his slight smile when, for the hundredth time, I emphasized the need for caution. It was a smile worldly, confident, and with a contradictory trace of innocence.

But he took to the training for his mission with an unmatched keenness. He loved the parachute training, and he wanted to keep on jumping long after his proficiency had been established. He loved the demolition work, the techniques of clandestine entry, and all the other cloak-and-dagger things. Only the code work did he find boring. He saw no reason why he should need to send us messages. He'd just go into Norway and raise hell, blow up everything the Germans wanted to keep, kill as many of them as he could, and survive as long as possible. It was all basic with Olaf.

He made Bergen his base. And as cover for his sabotage operations, he got himself a job as a docker. It gave him an excuse for being in the waterfront area, it was work he had done before, and it gave him, because of the sporadic nature of the employment, a certain freedom of movement for his real mission.

Olaf was operational for some three months after his first drop. We then brought him out for a few days of rest and briefing in London, and he was dropped again to continue his work. He couldn't wait to go back. He was like a racehorse honed to the keen edge of fitness, eager for the excitement of competition. It was difficult to believe that anyone who had been exposed to the tensions, the hardships, the danger and the treachery of wartime clandestine work could so obviously enjoy the work. And yet Olaf quite frankly chafed to get back to it all. Bravado? Yes, it was a certain bravado, but it was more than that, something difficult to describe, more difficult to comprehend. One could only be grateful for it and use it as we did in Olaf's case.

Olaf ranged the whole area between Bergen and Oslo as though it were his private domain. Anything German in that area at some time or other felt his touch. The rail lines were easy, and with his carefully organized and directed groups of workers, Olaf was able to keep the Germans almost constantly occupied with the repair of the lines. The rolling stock was also a basic target, and he whittled away at it incessantly.

There were moments. It wasn't all easy, uninterrupted or unsuspected. The Germans were constantly vigilant against saboteurs, but Olaf had been lucky, and though he had had a couple of near-misses, he had not been captured, nor was his identity known. It helps considerably if one's enemy doesn't know what he's looking for in the specifics of an individual.

Winter, with its heavy snows, made the hit-and-run type of sabotage operation almost impossible, especially in the isolated country areas. After all, tracks in the snow, whether ski marks or footprints, were an invitation to suicide.

Olaf moved his operations into town—Oslo.

Oslo offered plenty of scope. It was also infinitely more dangerous . There were "quislings" in Oslo, ready to turn on the most loyal Norwegian for a price, so that every contact, every plan, every operation, had to be approached with extreme caution. Basically Olaf was a solitary, which was to his advantage. All of his more spectacular jobs had been done almost single-handed, or at least with the minimum of assistance from the smallest number of accomplices. But he had a quality of leadership about him that he seemed not to recognize. The few who worked with him followed him blindly. It was as if they were infected with the virus of his own flamboyance, his own special brand of bravado, courage, and daring. It made for tight teamwork, as in the sabotage of the German billet in Bergen. Instinctively he trusted and worked with men of his own stamp, daring to the point of complete disregard for their own safety. They were tough. They were resilient. They were resourceful. They were loyal. These qualities he recognized and accepted quickly in his men.

His weakness was in his judgment of women. Or rather his lack of judgment. In a woman he seemed to demand only a good body, a pretty face, plenty of stamina, and a minimum of resistance. It gave a wide field.

Part of his problem in his relations with women rose from his ease of conquest. Women fell hard for his virile blond good looks, and because they were such easy prey he looked down on all women as "dumb broads". I remember his saying to me one day, "Women only have two emotions. They laugh or cry." It apparently never occurred to him that they also scheme and think.

Like Brita.

Who knows how they met? All we know is that they did meet and it was not, like so many of Olaf's conquests, a one-shot affair. Brita was sensual, and Olaf kept going back to her. Not that he gave up any others, he just kept Brita on his string as a kind of permanent playmate. It was a Nordically torrid liaison.

I learned this part of Olaf's story from Gunnar. Gunnar was Olaf's most trusted accomplice. It was Gunnar who had scrutinized the young German lieutenant in the small café in Bergen for Olaf. It was Gunnar who had knocked the German down with the spring cosh. It was Gunnar who had brought the explosives, fuses, and timers, wrapped and dry, for Olaf's use on that stormy night in Bergen. And it was Gunnar who had felt uneasy over Brita. There was something about her.

As he had said, most of Olaf's girls had been exactly as Olaf thought of all women. They came, they had a drink or perhaps a meal, they went to bed with him and, more often than not, he never saw them again. Certainly they never had anything to say beyond a kind of stupid patter, suggestive, aimed at exciting and luring and stimulating the male in him. It was all the usual rather pathetic parody of "making love". There was never any interest beyond the body and the moment. No one ever seemed to care what anyone was or what anyone did.

Except Brita. Brita asked questions, wheedled, probed. She wanted to know all about Olaf. She flattered him with her interest in his travels, his exploits in the Far East, the Middle East, and Europe. In short, she got him to talk.

Olaf was wary. And he was security-conscious. He was careful to give Brita no more than he gave to anyone else by way of explaining his life. He was an ordinary seaman, he insisted, and he had his cards to prove it. Beyond this he would not go. And when she tried to get him into a discussion of the Nazi occupation of Norway, when she urged him to give his own views, all she could get out of him was an intensely expressed hatred for the Germans and everything they represented.

Gunnar sat in on some of these evenings over a drink in a small café, and he was uneasy over the insistence that he sensed in Brita's pursuit of information. He had told Olaf of this feeling, and he had cautioned him. Olaf had laughed and replied that Brita was just a "dumb broad" like all the rest, only she talked more. Except when they were alone in bed. He laughed that he never gave her a chance to talk then, she'd be Goddamn lucky to be able to catch a breath.

It did not, however, interfere with his work for the OSS. Olaf continued his sabotage forays against the Germans in the Oslo area. With Gunnar and with other trusted companions whom he had carefully and tediously instructed in the wiles and techniques of the saboteur, Olaf attacked and destroyed equipment, storage depots, rolling stock, and in one spectacular foray, shipping. It was all effective.

He had overlooked one small chink in his security. Brita was demanding and possessive. She wanted him every night—all night—to herself, and she was petulant when he failed to appear on those nights when his raids took all of his attention. To anyone curious, to anyone interested enough to observe the pattern, it was not difficult to discover a direct relationship between Olaf's broken dates with Brita and an act of sabotage. To a casual observer there would be no significance. But Brita happened not to be a casual observer.

No one will ever known whether or not Olaf was already suspect as a saboteur by the Germans when Brita first came into his life and she was therefore an agent-provocateur, or whether Brita, on her own, had discovered the significance of the pattern and had tipped off the Germans. It really makes little difference now—the result was bound to be the same. All we know is that Olaf, brave and daring beyond the average but with a realist's nod toward security, was unknowingly under surveillance.

She was warm-soft against the muscled hardness of his lean body. It was that wonderful time when the frenzy, the urgent turmoil, and the final explosion had played their part. Everything was now serene, quiet, a blissful nirvana in a haze of contentment. They lay still conjoined and made small, caressing love play with their lips and their hands and fingers, searching and familiar in the dark silence of the room.

It was a faint, far-off shuffling sound when first heard. Only heard, but unregistered.

He held her closer to him as a kind of assurance that no other world existed.

It grew louder, the sound. Still without meaning, not yet identified or associated, it had a kind of disordered insistence, a threat of annoyance, a basic disturbing of the peace and quiet of his little haven. He listened now, more curious than anxious, listened and waited. The warm fullness of Brita's body, moist against him, acted like a soporific, for she seemed not to have heard.

Then, harsh, loud, the scraping, shuffling thump was there,

just beyond his door. It subsided for a moment, there was the muffled sound of guttural voices, and there was a loud rapping on the door, imperious, insistent to the point of banging.

With a soundless stealth he pushed himself away from the warm body that had been almost a part of him. She looked up at him quizzically, and he wondered at her calm. She was composed, undisturbed, unalarmed by the banging on the door, the loud voices. He could hear them distinctly now, the German commands. They were there, just outside the door, and yet this girl seemed unperturbed at the threat to their cosy sanctuary.

He slid away from her across the wide bed. His gun lay on a small table near at hand, and without taking his eyes off Brita, he groped for it, found it, and closed his fingers around it.

Suddenly he understood all. And he knew. It was her eyes. There was a taunt, a sly amusement, a "smarter-than-you" kind of insolence in them. The look was hard, contemptuous, defiant. Then, even as he watched, while he reached for and found his gun, the insolence turned to terror as she read his intent.

Her scream was shattered, unfinished, into silence.

They were forcing the door now, and even as her blood made crimson abstractions on the whiteness of the sheets, Olaf turned his gun on the door. He cross-hatched it up and down and sideways for good measure. There was answering gunfire from the hall, splintering the woodwork, pulverizing the plaster. In another moment they would be in the room.

There was no time for anything but escape. Olaf opened the small garret window and flung himself out. There was a drop of a few feet to the roof tiles below him, and in another moment he had slipped and skidded, clawed and pulled his way over a ridge and down to the protection of an adjacent roof. Everything was grey in the breaking dawn light; the roofs, the gables, the cornices, the menace of the streets three and four storeys below, it was a maze of forbidding danger.

His only hope was to get as far as possible from the room and to stay out of sight range of the window through which he had escaped. There was a small gable perched precariously on a steep roof, and he made for it not knowing where it led, what he would find, whether or not it would be a haven. He pulled himself up to the gable, forced the little casement windows, and hardly taking the precaution to look inside before going any farther, he crawled over the sill.

It was an attic, obviously unused. There were cobwebs and dust and soot-covered bales and boxes that looked as if they had been there a hundred years; a dim light was cast over everything from two or three other small windows. He moved quietly now. He had no idea what might be underneath, and he wanted time. Time to get his breath, time to think, time to plan his next moves.

He had not one shred of clothing with him. Not that it especially bothered him at the moment, but it would make his future moves more difficult.

He looked about him. There were a couple of dusty coverings thrown over some boxes, discarded draperies, old coverlets, it made no difference. He pulled one from the heap, shook the dust from it, and drew it around his naked body. He was cold, and the dusty protection of the tattered material felt not only warming but reassuring.

Olaf spent the next hour in the desperate torment of the hunted. Every tiny sound, every squeak, every scrape, every thump, no matter how distant, brought him to a tensed attention.

And he assessed his chances. He knew that his range of activity would be limited by the extent of the city block. At least as long as he kept to the roofs and buildings. He was also familiar enough with Nazi methods to realize that they would spare nothing to find him. Certainly, whatever they knew, if it had been important enough to bring them searching him out at four o'clock in the morning, they would never relax their search until he had been found. It was almost a certainty that there would be a building-by-building, room-by-room, attic-by-attic, and roof-by-roof search of the whole block. It would be equally certain that the block would be ringed with guards against any escape at ground level. He was desperate.

In one bright moment of hope he thought that his best chance, perhaps his only chance, would be to go back to his own room. He reasoned that the Nazis would have searched every cranny of the room and the areas and floors adjacent to it on their first entry to his quarters. They would have then taken anything they might think incriminating, and he was relieved to know that he had left nothing in his room to indicate any slightest involvement in sabotage, or other clandestine activity. He would, he decided with a certain confidence, go back to his room after dark, late at night.

He rolled himself tighter into his musty covering and tried to sleep. It was impossible. He was too much on edge, too aware of the danger he was in to relax, and he stayed fitfully, alternately on guard and relaxed for he knew not how long.

There had been few sounds of activity below him, and he wondered if he were perhaps in a building that was abandoned, only partially used, or perhaps a storage place. Then he heard them. The sound of footsteps, the voices, the scratching, prodding, probing, and thumping sounds of search. Silently, he drew far back into the darkest corner of the attic, under the eaves, pulled the coverlet completely over himself and rolled into a shapeless heap. It seemed to him that the very beating of his heart would be the giveaway. It crashed against his ears with an erratic pulsing so heavy it seemed it could be heard yards away.

A door opened in the distance. The voices were now louder, clearer, and he could understand the German commands, the comments—the heavy, menacing clump of the footsteps on the treads, the cautioning, one to the other, against any possible surprise assault.

Olaf re-gripped his gun.

Three? Four? He couldn't tell. Only the voices and the pounding of the feet, coming nearer and nearer to where he lay hidden.

He read their moods in the sounds. First the caution, then, on finding nothing, again nothing, the shuffled boredom of yet another building searched and yielding nothing. The kicking of a box here, a bale there, the perfunctory, now casual, scrutiny.

"Ach!"

The short, sharp exclamation brought everyone to attention, and Olaf held his breath and listened.

They had discovered marks where the dust had been disturbed. They were at the window, the window through which he had entered the attic; they discovered a clearly outlined bare footprint, and they were suddenly excited, alerted, advising each other, closing in.

In one wild moment he thought he would make a sudden break for it, throw off the covering and bolt. His saner, calmer self told him to stay quiet, that his only hope lay in the one slim chance that he might yet go undetected.

The excited talk had subsided, there were muffled exchanges that he couldn't make out, and he waited, alternately alarmed and elated. Perhaps at last he would make it.

Suddenly he was surrounded. They were clever, the Nazis. In one concerted action they surrounded him, drew the coverlet tighter around him, and held him encased in the dusty shroud. He fought frantically to free himself from the suffocating sack they had formed of his covering, but it was hopeless. In another moment they had hoisted him from the floor still in the heavy material and half lifted, half dragged him toward the stairs. His gun fell away from him in the mêlée, and one of the Germans grabbed it with a victor's shout. Then, when they found that the narrow staircase prohibited them from carrying their squirming bundle, they covered him with their guns, carefully uncovered his naked body, and ordered him to rise, hands aloft.

There, in the attic, they tied his wrists together with his hands behind his back, and with two Nazis preceding him and two following, they forced him down the three flights to the street. There was much excited talk with the guards outside the building about the capture, and then they were ready to take him in to Gestapo headquarters.

They taunted him about his girl friend, Brita. They made ribald comments about her descriptions of him. They contemptuously admitted that he was as handsome as she had described him, but they added, with much degenerate commentary, that they would have to take her word for it about his prowess in bed.

Then the perverted, depraved sadism so characteristic of the Nazi bullyboys showed itself. They led him naked through the streets of Oslo to Gestapo headquarters. His four captors walked with him in the grisly parade.

The Nazis apparently knew more about Olaf than he had thought possible. And they had apparently been watching him for some time. Or else their bluff was expert.

They held him for three days in the prison basement of their headquarters in Oslo. They were three days of hell. Constantly under the glaring probe of brilliant, blinding spotlights, twenty-four hours a day, he was never left alone. Then, periodically, he was taken out for questioning. Questioning and torture.

Blinding lights played into his eyes at these sessions so that he could never see his questioners, never identify the face that went with the voice. And then when the answers didn't come fast enough, or when they didn't reveal what was required, the tortures were applied.

Had he anything to do with the dynamiting of a certain ship? And when the answer was in the negative they tore out a fingernail with a pair of pliers. Or did he perhaps know something about the demolition of a certain shipment of strategic *matériel*? And when the reply was again a denial of a certain out another fingernail. What about the blowing of a certain bridge, the billet at Bergen, a drydock with a German ship under repair, what of these? In bleeding pain, sure of the reward for his answer, Olaf still refused to admit any part in the sabotage, and with each refusal they tore at his flesh, uprooted his fingernails, and left him with horribly mangled hands, half crazed with pain.

They tried to get him to identify his accomplices. Over and over again they questioned, pressured, tortured him for this information. They lashed him with bullwhips until he fell unconscious in a heap of bleeding pulp and they no longer could go on with the questioning and had to drag him back to his cell to recuperate.

They tried drugs. They gave him "truth serums", and they experimented with alternate shots of drugs to induce first elation and then depression, until he hardly knew or cared that he was living. Still he refused to break.

Suddenly they stopped. There was no explanation, no reason, only the sudden relief from the constant torment of questions and torture, questions and torture, questions and torture. All sense of time had left him and he lay in his cell in a state of semi-shock, semi-coma, grateful only for each hour of respite from their brutality.

Then, one night, they came for him again. They took him from his cell and led him back to the hated torture chamber, the small, high-walled room with its spotlights, its bare questioner's table, its hard chair, its torture table.

The disembodied voice behind the table, behind the lights, began again, but the tone was strangely softer, more disarming.

Immediately Olaf was on guard.

Some trick, some deception to lure him into giving away his secrets, only this could be back of the changed manner, the almost friendly tone of the questioning voice.

His interrogator asked if he had rested well. He asked if he was being fed regularly. And he wanted to know if his cell was comfortable. There was irony in this last. Olaf had been cast naked into a cell with a stone floor and no furniture or any covering. The only thing that separated his treatment from that of an animal was the presence of a pail to be used as a toilet. Other than that, he was caged like any animal in a zoo.

They were going to release him, said the voice behind the probing lights. Perhaps he had not been involved in any sabotage against the Third Reich, but they would make sure that it would be impossible for him ever again to hide out, to be inconspicuous, unmarked.

They forced him to the torture table, a flat steel contraption with wide straps and chains to hold his body inflexible. They placed him on his back, strapped him motionless at neck, chest, waist, arms, and legs. A vice-like arrangement clamped his head rigid, and in another moment they had branded him. With searing irons they burned a large swastika into each cheek until he screamed with the pain and the smoke and stench of burning flesh choked him to a convulsed sobbing.

Then, as if that were not enough, they slashed a deep gash across one side of his nose, laid open a nostril, and cut into his lip. That, they said, was for the girl Brita, whom he had killed, the girl who said that he was the handsomest man she had ever known. This would correct all that.

Olaf could hardly remember going back to his cell. All he remembered was being kicked awake some hours later, his face covered with caked, dried blood, his head throbbing with pain. A guard handed him a pair of heavy boots and told him to put them on, that he was going on a hike.

It was the first bit of covering of any kind he had seen since his capture, and he slid his feet into the boots. A sudden slash of pain cut into his toes and the soles of his feet, and he started to take off the boots. The guard cursed at him and made him pull them back on and lace them tightly in place. Then, without any other clothing, he was led from his cell. Every motion, every step was a searing agony of jagged pain.

Still undercover, still within the same building, they placed him in a car. There were two men in the front seat when he was pushed into the back, and there was a guard either side of him on the back seat. In another moment they were out in the streets of Oslo. It was night, he had no idea what time, and it was snowing. They drove rapidly through the city, and he tried to make out the streets, to orient himself. When they suddenly realized what he was doing, there was an exchange of curt comment and command among his co-passengers and in a moment he was blindfolded.

It was cold, and yet they made no effort to offer him warm covering against his nakedness. He sat and shivered between his guards, each wrapped in a heavy overcoat. No one spoke, and there was only the grind and hum of the car, the occasional sway and skid to hold him to reality.

For an hour—longer—it was like this. Then, with no word, no warning, they suddenly stopped. There was an opening and closing of doors, and he felt the stabbing blast of cold, searing against his bare flesh, as it forced into the car. Again the opening of doors, the cold, and short comments among the four Germans. They would turn the car around, here. Then they would be ready to leave quickly.

He felt the turning of the car, the spinning of the wheels, and then the stopping.

The doors were opened, his guards beside him moved away, and the next moment he was being dragged from the car. It wasn't till they had him outside that they took away the blindfold. It was black-dark except for the thin dual streams of light from the hooded beams of the car. It was snowing heavily, and it was bitterly cold, but mercifully there was no wind. The torture boots made it almost impossible for him to stand.

Then, with no more discussion, no comment, nothing, as if they were only too eager to be free of further involvement in the sordid business, the four Germans got back into the car and drove off.

Olaf was too relieved to be terrified by his plight. Naked, shivering to the point of an uncontrolled palsy, he sat quickly in a snowbank and tore off the accursed boots. His feet were bleeding pulps of shredded flesh, and he pulled the larger shards of glass, thin slivers, tiny jagged angles of glass from his feet. He plunged his feet into the cold, numbing softness of the snow and then, almost insane with relief, he fell back against the soft chill of the snowbank and closed his eyes.

Olaf had no recollection whatsoever of how he got to the little farmhouse. The whole nightmare of his lost wandering in the snow, naked, cut and bleeding as he was, mercifully had been erased from his mind. He only knew that he did find help. And kindness.

They kept him for several weeks, until his wounds had healed. He had suffered frostbite, and there was a time when it was feared that he might have to sacrifice at least one foot to avoid the threat of gangrene. It was a wonderful country family, and there were three strapping sons who were aching to get into the act against the Germans. Olaf's tortures only firmed their intentions, and he brought them along easily to become new and valuable recruits for his OSS sabotage groups.

He was only partially puzzled by his sudden release by the Nazis. And as he gained his strength, as he healed and he was able to see the whole thing clearly, their tactic was obvious. They were sure of him. They knew that he was an active saboteur and possibly a key leader in a network of saboteurs. They apparently had no other leads, however, and they had decided to let him loose in the hope that he would lead them unwittingly to his accomplices. Marked as he was by their disfigurement, he would be easy to check out should he appear anywhere in public. His only hope was that they had no idea as to his whereabouts at the moment, or even of his actual survival.

Through one of the young farm boys he made contact with Gunnar. He sent word that he would stay in hiding at the remote farmhouse, but wanted to talk with Gunnar and make plans for the future raids. The young farm boy brought Gunnar back with him for a couple of days' reunion.

Gunnar had been clever. He had, once he learned of Olaf's capture by the Germans, stepped up the sabotage operations in a deliberate effort to convince the Nazis that Olaf was of no importance to the sabotage effort. It may just have been a factor in Olaf's release. At any rate, it added a nice bit of additional trouble for the Germans. And it kept Gunnar and his accomplices active.

Olaf gave Gunnar the complete rundown on the whole story, Brita's treachery, his escape, capture, questioning and torture, his final release. He admitted his ineptitude in putting trust in Brita, and then added, rather sadly but with a tone that attempted flippancy, that he had given up women for life, or rather women would give him up from now on, with the face he had.

Gunnar turned away from the shiny, taut-pink swastika scars on the formerly clear cheeks, the gashed lip and nostril where the fine mouth and handsome nose had been. There was nothing to say.

One of the most remarkable things about Olaf and his whole mission was the fact that the Nazi capture and torture in no way acted as a deterrent. If anything his experience only strengthened his hatred of the Germans and his resolve to harass them in every way possible. But it made him more cautious.

Through the rest of the winter of 1943–44, Olaf stayed in semi-hiding. He took a less active part in the actual sabotage operations, leaving the bulk of the work to Gunnar while he occupied himself with the planning. Where to strike, how to do each type of sabotage, how many and whom to use as personnel, these things Olaf handled from his hidden mountain retreat. He also contributed his incredible spirit. Though he had been tortured almost to the death, though he had been disfigured horribly for life and carried the hated stigma of the swastika branded on his face, he still had unconquerable courage.

There was a light touch to Olaf's brand of courage. Perhaps it verged on the flippant, perhaps it smacked of bravado, perhaps it was a trifle the manner of a cinema buccaneer, but whatever it was, it was a quality that was infectiously absorbed by all of the men who worked with him. They sensed his assurance and were themselves assured. It made for a tight group and high morale. It also made for successful operations.

Twice we suggested that we bring him into London for rest and re-orienting. Always he refused. Anything he needed, he insisted, by way of rest or change he could get in Norway. He sent Gunnar to us instead.

There were perhaps two reasons for his action in this regard. He suggested that it would be dangerous to the security of his whole mission and to the persons with whom he worked to run the risk of returning to London. And maybe he was right. If the Nazis were watching him, it would be a safe guess that they would know of any such movement. Discovery of such contact would undo all the hidden work he had accomplished since his release.

The other reason was more personal, and it was put forward by Gunnar. Gunnar was certain that Olaf did not want any of us in London to see his disfigurement. On his recommendation we no longer pressed for Olaf's return.

Then, with the beginning of spring and the fullness of summer, Olaf and his men stepped up their sabotage operations against the Germans in Norway. And when he could stand the inactivity no longer, when the fever of excitement reached the bursting point, Olaf began to take an active part in the raids himself.

He moved back to Bergen and went back to a job on the waterfront. It was a good cover, and he was clever in its use. He reasoned that the Germans would never believe that, marked as he now was, he would dare become involved again in active sabotage. Olaf nurtured this line of thought. For weeks he stuck only to his job. He had no direct contact with Gunnar, but worked only and sporadically through cut-outs so devious it would have been impossible for him to have been traced. He moved openly and boldly on the waterfront, taking special care to be seen in bars and cafés frequented by Germans as a proof that he had nothing to hide. He was slowly, painstakingly, rebuilding a solid base of freedom from suspicion.

He was still the mastermind.

The demolition of a supply depot? Olaf planned the whole thing to the last detail, worked out the alternatives in case there had to be a sudden shift of plan, and mapped out the escape pattern. Then, at the very hour when the scheme was to be put into effect, he himself was conspicuously present at some public place where there would certainly be many Germans. So much for his surveillance, and *that* for Adolf Hitler!

It worked. All through that summer and into the autumn, Olaf and Gunnar organized and activated their sabotage raids. But what he really longed for, what he really enjoyed and lived for, was the danger, the challenge, the excitement of being in the thick of it. Without that, there was no zest.

Twice we had had serious losses. The first time, the Germans had surprised one of our sabotage teams, a group of three, in the act of destroying a central power station. There was a running gun battle in the best Hollywood manner, and we lost two of the three men to the Germans; the third made good his escape. The second time, an underwater sabotage team of two men had been dispatched to sink a German naval vessel in the harbour at Oslo. They were using limpets, the barnacle-like explosive devices that clung magnetically to the underside of a ship and were activated by a timing mechanism. Their mission was a success in that the ship was sunk, but the two men were never seen again. They must have been the victims of their own work through some miscalculation of the timer or a similar malfunction.

These misfortunes preyed on Olaf, and he took them as a kind of reproof for his own inactivity. They were the final spur that drove him into the field again, fully committed.

In spite of anything Gunnar could say or do, Olaf plunged into a frenzy of activity. He seemed to have no regard for his own safety. Where he had always been daring and courageous, he was now reckless and defiant. More and more he planned one-man operations, operations of such daring and imagination, such delicacy and complexity, they seemed impossible. And always he was the one man to carry through with the operation.

More than ever he wanted and planned attacks against personnel, hoping always for another coup such as his demolition of the Nazi billet in Bergen. Supplies, *matériel*, fuel, power, these of course should be destroyed, but Olaf developed a blood lust to take as many Germans as possible with these other strategic targets. It was one more way of avenging the tortures and disfigurement he had suffered at the hands of the master race.

There was a favourite drinking spot in Olso that had been taken over completely by the Germans and where they brawled and drank late into the night. It was staffed by quislings, haunted by women sympathetic to the German forces, and ripe for action. Olaf decided to make the action.

This time there would be none of the drama or the good fortune of impersonating a German officer. With his tell-tale scars, that would be impossible. But he thought it through and he was so jealous of his plan, so sure of himself, he refused absolutely to give Gunnar the slightest hint of how he planned to wreck the café. He told Gunnar that he had a plan, that he would carry it forward, and that it would be successful. He would not describe it, nor would he tell when it would be brought off.

"You'll know it when," was all that he would say.

Then suddenly one day there was the rumour. And there were the facts to back it up. The café had been wrecked. A bomb? A grenade? A booby trap? Every type of sabotage was reported, and yet no one knew for sure. They only knew that there had been a sizable casualty list, and the feeling in Oslo at the time greeted it as an item of the most wonderful news. It had cleaned out quislings and Germans, too good to be true.

Gunnar had not seen Olaf for a couple of days prior to the sabotaging of the café, and now he waited for contact. He didn't expect it immediately. That would have been the wildest kind of folly; but he was sure that, given a week, perhaps two, Olaf would be in touch and he would have the story.

Two weeks. Three weeks. A month. There was no word. Gunnar could only wait and hope. Then as winter came on and there was still no word from Olaf, Gunnar signalled us the news in London that he was presumed lost. Captured? Dead? In hiding? Only the last seemed improbable.

We sat in the elegant luxury of the terraced dining-room of the Grand Hotel in Stockholm. The "Venice of the North" was all around us, and the glazed calm of the water made it look like so much quicksilver. I had flown in from the bleak austerity of London, where cream, eggs, butter, sugar, and the like were things one only spoke of, almost never saw. Gunnar, across the table from me, had come in from Norway, and the same gloomy, spare, haunted life, only worse—a country under enemy occupation—lay behind him. We both exclaimed over the wonder of it all again and again, and even while we revelled in the orgy of abundance, we felt the prick of guilt about it, knowing what lay behind and ahead of us.

It was then I got the finale to Olaf's story.

Parts of it Gunnar couldn't vouch for, because there was so much rumour. But what he did piece together was dramatic, if true. And knowing Olaf as we did, we thought it was certainly in character. The gist of it was that Olaf had quite simply walked into the little café on that fatal evening, taken a table, and had a couple of drinks. When he found the place well filled with the hated Nazis, he had paid for his drinks, risen from his chair, and started for the door. At the entrance, so the story went, he had turned, shouted for attention, and cursed

Hitler and the Third Reich. Before anyone in the room could react, he had tossed a grenade and bolted.

He had been captured almost as he left the building by two surprised Germans who were about to enter. All that, said Gunnar, was hearsay. And though he could not prove it, he could not disprove it, either.

The facts that he did have, the things that were known, were more grisly. Olaf had apparently been taken alive and had been held a prisoner for many weeks. They were undoubtedly weeks of the most incredible tortures. The Germans never seemed to be able just to kill—they had to torture first, kill by degrees and inches, as brutally as possible.

The demon that drove them to ever more horrible methods of inspiring terror worked overtime in this case. They had held Olaf until there had been another act of sabotage. It happened to be the ambushing of a German patrol on the outskirts of a small town in the mountains.

The next morning, in the little public square of the town, Olaf's nude body was found hanging. His body bore the marks of severe beatings, and he had been castrated. There was worse. The Nazis, in their fiendish sadism, had utilized two meat hooks. They were like two enormous fish-hooks, and they had been inserted just at the base of each ear in the soft part of the neck to the rear of the jaw. A living body, suspended on these torture hooks, slowly, by its own weight, forced the steel points into the brain.

It was in this manner that the "Master Race" had brought death to a young patriot.

We sat long at table that night in Stockholm, Gunnar and I. And a great part of the time was spent in silence, watching the glitter of the lights. They seemed so unreal after the blackout of London, and they were so out of keeping with our mood.

We tried recalling all of the crazy, bold, daring things that Olaf had done, to lighten the story of his death, but it was no good. We said good night and went off to bed.

I saw Gunnar the next day before I left to go back to London. He was cheerful again, eager to get back to Bergen and then on to Oslo. There was still much that could be done against the Germans, and he was more determined than ever to carry through the work that Olaf had directed and inspired. And I can remember his saying that he would never rest until he had at least one more German life to pay for what they had done to Olaf.

I never saw him again.

We had contact for a few weeks after I got back to London. The sabotage groups were still at work, and the Nazis were still being harassed at every turn. Then suddenly, there was that dread silence. It went on and on until it was no longer surprising but accepted.

I knew what it meant.

CHAPTER FIVE

ALICIA

FOR the most part the various agent operations of the OSS during World War II were tedious, slogging, lonely, and desperately dangerous assignments. Devoid of glamour, charged with uncertainty and anxiety, anonymous and unacknowledged, the real-life operation of the secret agent is as unlike the cinema and fiction versions offered the public as one could possibly imagine. Lush blondes, champagne suppers, soft lights, instant sex and flight, fast cars and planes, all this is Hollywood, caviar as against the real-life ham and eggs. James Bond, had he ever been involved in a real-life espionage assignment and operated in his flamboyant manner, would have been liquidated halfway through his first mission. The successful real-life agent, the one who does a masterly job and lives to go on to other assignments, rides a bus. He does not make himself conspicuous with custom-built motor cars.

Mata Hari, the World War I dancer-actress who became a spy and, through legend, has become the epitome of espionage glamour, was perhaps more successful as a courtesan than as an agent. The very fact that she had such a good press might indicate minimal espionage value. Who could know?

Out of the hundreds of agents operated by the OSS there was perhaps one whose type of mission came anywhere near the glamour assignments so beloved of the cinema and fiction. We called her Alicia.

Alicia had an exotic background to begin with, and her appearance was stamped with it. She was the daughter of an Englishman and a Parsee, that handsome group of pale-skinned, dark-eyed Indians found in and around Bombay and Baroda, descendants of Persians who fled to India in the eighth century.

With pale, pale, almost translucent skin, black eyes and blue-black hair, finely cut features and a good figure, she was the kind of woman other women called "interesting looking" when they found it impossible to admit that another of their sex might just possibly be beautiful. Men were more frank – they called her beautiful.

Everything was right. The bone structure was fine, the ankles and feet small, the languid hands accented with elegantly long fingers, the kind of hands that make most women reel with jealousy because they take to fine jewels as if born with them. This was Alicia.

I don't know anything of her early background and schooling, but it must have been worldly. She acted, quite naturally, as if all the world were her home, not just some tiny corner of it, and, to a great extent, it was. She was a blend of East and West, as easy to picture in the soft flowing folds of a sari as in the mannish tweeds of the English countryside. And why not? She had been exposed to both worlds. There had been an early marriage with a young Englishman, but that had ended after a short time, and then there had been a much better marriage with an older man, again an Englishman; with it there had been a title, a large country house, a London flat, and the sort of life that went with all that prior to the war. By the time she came onto the OSS pay-roll, she was out of England and married to a Swede, a man of position and wealth.

Throughout a war one is confronted with the wildest possible inconsistencies, the most improbable incongruities. Not the least of these involved the sudden transition from the immediate midst of war to the tranquil luxuries of peace. For weeks I had lived with bombs, fire, ack-ack, sirens, and destruction and death, the constant, gnawing harassments of rationing and shortages. Then suddenly all was luxury, peace, abundance, and sybaritic ease.

Lisbon.

Perhaps nowhere in the world has there ever been a hotel more suffocatingly opulent than the Aviz in Lisbon. Built originally as a private town house, it was run with all the deft elegance and thoughtfulness of a Parisian *hôtel particulière*. Accommodating some thirty guests in private suites with balconies giving on to the pastel roofs of Lisbon and the water beyond, with the finest of foods and wines and impeccable service, it was, after wartime London, like reaching nirvana.

It was there that I met Alicia for the first time.

She was already working for us, and I knew much about her. I'm sure she knew much about me. And yet our first introduction was as chill, as icily correct and disinterested, as if I had been just another waiter bringing drinks.

We were eight at lunch. Two men from the American Embassy, Alicia's current husband, the Swede, and I made up the male contingent. Alicia, a Swedish sister-in-law, and two American Embassy wives were the women. It was only my second day in Lisbon, and I was not yet accustomed to the tables of Germans, Italians, Japanese—every one who could be called enemy—so close at hand. Alicia took them all with an ignoring calm.

She was elegantly dressed, understated and carefully jewelled with only one or two authoritative pieces. But the most striking thing about her was the complete lack of make-up. The porcelain-pale skin, the dark eyes, the black hair—there was not the slightest attempt to accentuate them with the usual glistening scarlet gash of lipstick, or any tricks with the eyes, none of the green or blue shadow stuff, the liners, the added lashes, which somehow only serve to make women grotesque rather than beautiful. These Alicia did not need, and she was obviously clever enough to realize it.

For six out of the eight people grouped around the table at the Aviz that day, it was just one more lunch, no more memorable, no more unusual, no more exciting than hundreds of other hotel lunches bringing together eight people for the first time. But for me, and for Alicia, it was the beginning of a contact that was to continue throughout the war and to prove to be more than profitable for the OSS.

It had all been arranged by General Donovan. The General loved intrigue; he loved the secrecy, the plot and counterplot of espionage; and especially he loved the challenge of the seemingly impossible. Where or how he had first met Alicia I do not know; but I did learn from him that he had known her for some time prior to the outbreak of the war, that they had been close friends from the time of her second marriage, to the Englishman of title, and that he had himself recruited her to work for the OSS. Her reports were to him alone; but, as he was finding the demands of a growing espionage network more challenging, he found it necessary to make Alicia known to someone else to whom she might turn should he be unavailable. I was picked to be that someone.

Obviously the General could not introduce us, even privately, without running the risk of breaking security and killing Alicia's value to the OSS. And, as he told me long after the war was over, it was his own idea to remain in Washington, pull a few inconspicuous strings, and bring Alicia and me together at the table in Lisbon. He seemed especially delighted with the thought that neither our host, an officer of the American Embassy in Lisbon, nor Alicia's husband had the slightest inkling that she was a clandestine operative of the OSS and that I was the man handling the financing of those operations.

As a Swedish businessman, Alicia's husband moved easily about the world with his neutral passport. She moved with him. And since they had wide contacts in that international world that is part social, part financial, part diplomatic, part business, Alicia had a potential to the OSS as a secret agent that intrigued the imagination. To General Donovan it was irresistible. It was therefore, perfectly logical that she might be sitting at lunch in Lisbon with a group from the American Embassy.

Alicia knew why she was there. I knew why I was there. To the others it could only have been routine—the kind of chatter-lunch where one heard that Freddy had been shot down over Germany, such a pity, he had been so good at polo, and then went on to chaff about the rationing situation in England, the war-bond drives in New York, and related inconsequentials.

When we shook hands and said good-bye after the lunch was over, it was all done with a casualness that belied our involvement.

To the layman, to anyone unfamiliar with the ways and means of espionage, it may be incomprehensible just how a woman in Alicia's position might be of any positive intelligence value. True, some highly important and vital military secrets may be picked up all of a piece and delivered by a single agent in a neatly certified package. But, unfortunately, much of the most delicate intelligence, and often much of the most important, comes piecemeal; the whole story is only worked out like a jigsaw puzzle, a bit at a time. One agent, operating quietly in a remote area, may send in some significant bit of information that has no real value of itself; then another agent may produce some related bit; an interesting and significant pattern may appear with yet another item from a third source; but still there may be nothing definite enough to merit action. Then, often unexpectedly and from an improbable source, may come the key snippet of detail that completes the picture; and suddenly we know exactly what the enemy is up to in the situation at hand. Quite obviously anyone with perceptive intelligence, language facility, and a certain freeedom of movement in the higher echelons of society and the diplomatic world can be of tremendous value in finding the missing pieces to many an espionage puzzle. Evidence of the value of the casual remark is the fact that one of the great intelligence services of the world for years placed clandestine agents in the salons of an internationally known cosmetics chain. The offhand gossip of embassy wives about who is where, who is expected where, who is up and who is down, all of this is grist to the mill, often indicating vitally important shifts in power, political emphasis, and the like, of the country in question.

Alicia had this value. And more.

Fluent in several languages, at home in all of the major capitals of the world, with friends widely scattered in the Allied, the enemy, and the neutral camps, Alicia had a value to be treasured. She also had great perception, keen intelligence, and a disarming gaiety that gave everything she said and did a light touch. It could have been a cultivated frivolity. Nor did it harm her value to the OSS in the least that she was also strikingly handsome. Even the most rigorously trained and disciplined espionage agent in the world finds it difficult to resist such a woman.

It was months before I saw her again.

But I heard from her regularly. With the General and with Alicia, although we at no time met to discuss the situation, we worked out a system of communication that, even at this late date, should not be described in detail. It should be enough to say that, through existing confidential international offices of impeccable discretion, we were able, Alica and I, to keep in secure communication. These offices would have been startled to discover that they were a link in an effective espionage chain, and even today they would no doubt find it difficult to credit.

From Stockholm, from Geneva and Berne, from Lisbon,

Madrid, and Istanbul, Alicia sent in her gleanings on the more involved foreign operations of the Axis powers. And the names flowed through her reports like a roster of the enemy great—von Papen, Schacht, Goebbels, Goering, Dietrich, Ciano, Graziani, Badoglio, and countless others. Some she had met and exchanged pleasantries with, others she had only seen at gatherings; but all, in some way or other, had furnished just a bit more background to the myriad details that helped us to fill in the picture of what was really happening in the midst of the enemy camp.

Then came the word that it was urgent that we meet to discuss a possible change in her plans and operating methods. It was a chancy thing, this. So far there had been no open record of our contact, nothing whereby an enemy snooper could trace a line from Alicia to me to the General, or any variation on the theme. She and General Donovan had not met for months, and except for our innocent introductory lunch in Lisbon, she and I had not even been in the same country at the same time. This new suggestion, that we meet and discuss further plans, was disturbing; but in view of the fact that our present arrangement was working well and producing, it was obvious that her suggestion was prompted by some hidden urgency.

I discussed the problem with General Donovan, and he agreed that I should meet with Alicia as she requested. He hardly needed to add that the meeting should be most discreet and as innocent of prearrangement as possible. It worked even more smoothly than I could have imagined.

Alicia flew into England "to stay with relatives in the country". I "happened" to be a weekend guest at another English country house a few miles away. And there just happened to be a race meeting not too far from either one.

It was as if no war existed.

Everything that could be used as a conveyance and still meet with the petrol-rationing curbs was on the road. And one very prominent and rather eccentric English racing fan had herself propelled by barge up the river to a landing not too far from the course. There were the picnic hampers, the good-looking women in tweeds, the men on leave in country clothes, and a good smattering of uniforms from the Allied nations as well as the British.

There was the paddock and the horses—sleek bays, browns,

chestnuts, and greys and blacks. The glint of bit and buckle. The bright stab of the silks, scarlets, greens, blues, yellows, and purples, against the manicured green of the turf, the lush, protective awning of the old trees.

There, quite informally and quite by "accident" our separate groups met, Alicia's and mine. There were the usual mumbled English introductions that are no introductions at all, a sort of "do you know Lord Tiddlypush, Commander Blank, Lady Shankhannon, the Hon. Mrs. Watshername," until it has all trailed off into nothingness, odd grunts and smiles and clipped "hodgeejews" or blank stares; and then everyone can relax back into the serious business of picking a winner for the next race.

Alicia and I were caught up in it all, casually and unmarked. And there, leaning on the paddock rail, race cards in hand, pencils ready, we had our rendezvous.

She was looking handsome, even more so than I had remembered her from Lisbon. But there was a difference. Where she had looked exotic and excitingly worldly in the international background of wartime Lisbon, here, at an English race meeting, she looked like any other well-bred, elegantly tweeded, strikingly good-looking Englishwoman. It rather underscored her value to us.

What she had to say was a shocker.

She was leaving her Swedish husband. Without going into detail, she told how the marriage had been going from bad to worse and said she was sure her husband was suspicious of her activity. He had said nothing directly to indicate it; but there were inferences, innuendoes that made her uneasy. This, coupled with the fact that she had sensed, in his carefully professed neutrality, a tentative leaning toward the Axis cause, had prompted her to seek advice. Personally she wanted to leave him; the marriage as such was finished, and there was no one else. But what she hesitated to do was to break up a highly successful and, for her, lucrative, espionage operation if it was felt that she could safely continue in her present course.

With her usual keen perception and foresight, she had an alternative. She had met in Stockholm and become quite friendly with a young German colonel. It was a purely innocent friendship; but, such was her hold over the young man, she had persuaded him to take her to Paris for a weekend against the wishes of her husband. It was a perfectly innocent weekend, done as a lark and to be able to say to her friends in Stockholm that she had just been in Paris for a few days. But it had awakened her to possibilities that were fascinating in their implication.

In short, this remarkable woman Alicia was prepared quite calmly and coolly to abandon her husband, whom she admittedly no longer loved, and to take a chance on setting herself up in Paris as the mistress of a young German colonel. It was only for the General and myself to decide which course would be of the greater value to the OSS.

I pointed out to her the hazards of her present position, and I emphasized the fact that her danger as a kept woman in Paris would be incredibly increased. In her present status she had freedom to move from country to country in a manner denied to most individuals in a world at war. In German-occupied Paris, in the shadow world of an officer's mistress, she would be restricted to the whims of the Nazi bosses and subjected to the constant surveillance of the Gestapo. The disturbing factor in the whole complicated picture was the fact that her husband might just possibly be a pro-Nazi neutral. If he were that and at the same time suspicious of her and ready to write finis to a stumbling marriage, it could mean the end of her effective work for the OSS in its present form; and, worse, it might even mean a threat to her very life.

It was a wildly incongruous meeting.

The saddling paddock. The arrival of each new group of sleek, lithe young horses, the colour and the subdued excitement, the parade to the post, the last-minute scramble to place a bet, the race, the cheers and moans, and again the paddock and the candidates for the next race. With all this as background, in instalments and snippets, I got Alicia's story. And I agreed to discuss the whole problem in detail with General Donovan at the earliest possible moment.

Alicia went back to her relatives and then on to Stockholm. I returned to London.

The General's pale-blue eyes sparkled as he listened to my presentation of Alicia's suggestions. If there was anything the General enjoyed more than intrigue, it was intrigue spiced with generous lashings of *l'amour*. With those quick jerks of his head, the steady man-to-man stare that always indicated full concentration, he listened to the whole story of my talk with Alicia. Then he began thinking out loud, as he so often did, making a kind of verbal first draft of his final decision. He weighed very carefully the value of Alicia's reports to date; and, listed as they were, simply and concisely, they were remarkably rewarding. A final separation and divorce from her husband might completely dry up her sources, meaning a definite loss to the OSS.

On the other hand, the idea of Alicia's operating from occupied Paris, in close contact with the German military, had a certain fascination for the General. As well he knew, we already had good, reliable, and productive agents in Paris. But always in clandestine operations one hopes to cover every possible angle, and there is a natural hesitation in not taking advantage of every opportunity for expansion. In Paris she could be tremendously effective, but with limited scope. But with the shaky condition of her marriage, with the threat of a suspicious and possibly pro-German husband, might not her scope for Stockholm become equally limited? Perhaps, he mused, we had best accept the fact that, as an effective secret agent, Alicia no longer had the value to the OSS she once had had.

Then he made his decision. And looking back on it now, I know it was the only logical decision for this man of action, of intrigue, of danger and courage, to make. He thought Alicia would be of greatest value to the OSS if she continued in her present position but with the added dimension of probing the possibilities of further sorties into occupied Paris. Or even, and his eyes widened with the excitement of it, into Berlin itself. After all, if she *had* a pro-German husband, what better way to deaden his suspicions of her as an Allied agent than to have her go to Germany under the sponsorship of a German officer? It *could* be done.

He emphasized the fact that the decision would have to be hers, Alicia's, to make. All I was to do was to instruct her as to the merits of the alternatives and suggest that she might possibly wish to stay with her husband while cultivating the young German colonel for what he could offer. As a man of the world, the General saw no reason why an attractive woman might not openly maintain the security and position offered by a good marriage, even though that marriage was finished, and at the same time, with discretion, benefit from the possibilities of a liaison.

Alicia met the challenge.

It was the beginning of a frighteningly dangerous charade. It called for cool nerves, infinite patience, and diabolical deception. To be an agent in enemy territory is to live constantly with danger. But to be an agent, and at the same time to be married to someone who may be suspicious of one's activities, then to compound that with the possibility that the spouse is sympathetic to the other side, is to live a nightmare.

Alicia built a new foundation to her whole mission. To the exclusion of almost everything else she worked on her husband. The marriage was finished; but she kept up the pretence of a normal marriage and she began, little by little, to win back her husband's confidence. Not once had there been mention of her sympathy to the Allied cause, although she had English relatives, English background, and many Allied friends, English, French, American. But so, also, she had many Germans, Italian, and other nationalities among her associates. Living in the neutral atmosphere of Sweden made it relatively easy for her to keep in touch with them all, and she began a deft shift of emphasis toward the Axis contacts of her husband.

She played on his business sense and suggested that, since she had many English contacts, the flow of business in that direction was assured. It might be well to cultivate the young German colonel and perhaps increase her husband's business dealings with the Axis powers. The small dinner parties began to include more of the Axis world in Stockholm; and, more often than not, the young German colonel was there. The trips to the neutral countries, to Switzerland, to Spain and Portugal, to Turkey, these continued; and there was one more sortie into Paris, this time with her husband included. Except for the preponderance of Nazi uniforms and the display of the hated swastika everywhere, it was almost like a peacetime visit to *la ville lumière*.

Gradually her confidence expanded. On the personal side there seemed to be a lessening of tension between herself and her husband. Certainly there was an increasing rapport with the young German colonel. He had long been under Alicia's spell; but more and more he ingratiated himself with her husband, until they became a happy, confiding threesome. It was a threesome in which each had some special motive. Alicia sought information. The young German colonel sought more goods for Germany; and he no doubt sought, or at least hoped for, favours from Alicia. Her husband sought trade, the expanded, profitable, two-way street of dealing with both enemy camps, the Allies and the Axis. The way to the Axis could be augmented through a closer relationship with the German colonel.

With the skill of a now experienced agent, Alicia nurtured this three-sided friendship. Then, when the time was right, she made her play for the supreme target – Berlin.

It was a black Mercedes from the German Embassy that drove them out to Bromma, the large and busy airfield on the outskirts of Stockholm. Alicia sat between her husband and the young German colonel. A representative of the *Sicherheitsdienst*, the SD or German security police, a branch of the Gestapo, sat in front beside the liveried chauffeur. The SD man was in plain clothes, an unexpected and unsettling addition to the party. He was there when the car had pulled up in front of their house in Stockholm; he had alighted, along with the German colonel, and held the door for Alicia as she entered the car; and he assisted with the luggage. But his presence had limited the conversation to comments on the weather, flight times, and other banalities, as they drove to the field.

The huge Lufthansa plane was already on the ramp before the terminal building. For one quick chilling moment Alicia felt fear quiver in her body as she saw the menacing black swastika on the plane and realized that, within minutes, she would be leaving the freedom of Sweden behind and would be completely at the mercy of the fanatical Nazis.

The sleek Mercedes eased toward a special gate, the SD man flashed a special pass, and as the gates were opened, the car moved forward across the ramp and came to a stop at the very base of the steps to the plane. A couple of Swedish officers (Alicia guessed they might have been a security control) saluted as she stepped from the car, and she smiled and thanked them. Then, as the luggage was quickly shifted from car to plane, Alicia, her husband, the young German officer, and the SD man entered the plane and took a group of choice seats that had been reserved for them. They had little engraved cards on them with the seal of the German Embassy in Stockholm heavily embossed.

All other passengers were in place, and the plane was filled. Germans, Italians, they were obviously there. There may have been other nationalities, and Alicia strained to catch a phrase, another tongue perhaps, but her efforts were killed by the sudden ignition of the tremendous motors. Then, as if time were vital, they were on the runway, there was a momentary check, there was the tremendous roaring, thrusting forward lunge of the plane, and they were airborne. Straight, no banking, no turning, no circling over the sparkling waters and gleaming buildings of Stockholm, but straight over the city, over the Baltic, straight for Germany.

They were high, too high to mark any details, as they flew over the north German plains, and by the time they were over Tempelhof, the field for Berlin, there was a heavy overcast and silver slashes of rain were cutting across the windows of the plane. Once again there was no nonsense about circling but a straight run in, a fast landing, and a screeching halt at the end of the runway. As the plane taxied back to the terminal building a young steward in uniform appeared from the cockpit and announced that all passengers would remain in their seats until they were given further orders to disembark.

The plane had swung into position on the ramp, the motors were cut, and now the door was being opened and the steps locked into place. Two men in SD uniform entered the plane, saluted the young German colonel, and spoke to the SD man in plain clothes accompanying Alicia and her party. They were polite but coldly official, and they asked Alicia to follow them from the plane.

She felt slightly tense as she walked to the door, but her husband was close behind her, the German colonel was there smiling, and at the foot of the steps waited another large black-and-silver Mercedes. It was flying a red, black, and white pennant from each front fender with the hated swastika.

They were seven in the car for the ride into Berlin – Alicia, again on the back seat between her husband and the German colonel, her own private plain-clothes SD man on a jump seat, and one of the uniformed SD men beside him, the other uniformed SD man in front beside the chauffeur.

Already the little patterns of Nazi power were beginning to show. The talk was strained and banal, subdued; but there was the obvious awareness of rank. The plain-clothes SD man quite obviously outranked the two in uniform, as was shown by the deference with which they treated him. They all three were cautiously respectful and attentive to the young colonel;

and, yet, Alicia sensed a certain underlying contempt for him on the part of all three SD men. It did not make for a happy entry into the city.

Alicia's husband was on a business trip. And when she had first suggested to the young German colonel that she would like to accompany him to Berlin, she had been told that would be impossible. She had worked on the idea incessantly with the colonel; and then, quite suddenly, without any further explanation, she had been told that she might go with her husband the following day. They would be allowed to remain in Berlin for three days only. And now they were there.

Yet it hardly seemed probable that the special treatment they were accorded was routine for all business visits to war-time Berlin from neutral countries. The embassy car in Stockholm, the special seats, the preferred debarkation treatment in Berlin, and again the car and the complete clearance of the usual customs controls—how could they all be explained if it were not for the fact that the SD was so prominently active? It was Alicia's guess, and she was probably most certainly correct, that the Germans had a full dossier on her, that they were well aware that her father had been English, that she had had two English husbands, and that she had been only recently in England. It was further possible that they thought she might be of some value to them because of this background. The Swedish husband, trading with them, might this not be good security against any treachery on her part?

The fact that they were undecided about Alicia is underlined by the constant SD surveillance. And just in case there might be any doubt about that, the hotel arrangements for Alicia and her husband should clinch the point. They were lodged in a suite of sitting-room, double bedroom, and bath; but the young colonel was in a single room on one side of the suite, and the private, plain-clothes SD man was in a single room on the other side of the suite. It was a cosy arrangement for everyone except Alicia.

The Germans were thorough, if nothing else. Not once during the three days in Berlin did Alicia and her husband go out alone. Her husband's business conferences and contacts were constantly shadowed and openly attended by the SD man. Alicia had the more charming company of the young German colonel—but never alone. Whether they went for a sketchy sightseeing trip, carefully stage-managed to avoid the worst-damaged sections of the city, or a shopping trip of the false-fronted shops, a visit to the Potsdamerzee, or an ersatz lunch, Alicia and the colonel were invariably accompanied by one or two other people. It was a wearing experience.

What made it even more unbearable was the fact that Alicia had discovered, soon after her arrival at the hotel, that the suite was "bugged". Sitting-room, bedroom, bathroom, not a sound, a word, but that someone, perhaps the colonel or the SD man, could hear, perhaps even record.

There was more. Each time they left the suite, someone had made a methodical search of their personal belongings and their luggage, until Alicia was certain there was not a seam, not a lining, not an article of clothing, a hairbrush, a pencil, but had been searched and probed by Nazi agents.

They could have saved themselves the trouble. In the first place Alicia had trained herself to rely on her memory. She made no notes, she carried no incriminating memoranda or letters, and there was nothing else that could possibly indicate her true activity as an operating agent of the OSS. But as she later said, even had there been any tendency in this direction it would have been quickly smothered by the intense surveillance accorded her by the Nazis.

Three days later Alicia was safely back in Stockholm. And within the week General Donovan had her first report from Berlin. It was a background report, of necessity, but it revealed much of value. The obvious success of Allied bombing raids could not be hidden, and she reported the destruction of several specific targets. The use of huge nets appliquéd with simulated leaves and branches and spread over crucial buildings in an attempt to make the centre of the city look like a park, this she reported. The scarcities in the shops, the desperate attempts to keep up a front of normality in the face of increasing shortages and hardships. The general appearance and attitudes of the crowds in the streets showing the strain of being constantly in the middle, attacked by an enemy and at the same time suspect, watched, harried by their own government. All this came through from Alicia.

There were added dividends.

So obviously correct had been Alicia's conduct in Berlin (and perhaps because her husband did have a value to the Nazi war cause) that there were three more short trips into Berlin. Always there was the special service. But the surveillance became less obvious with each trip, although it could be felt, hidden and sinister.

On one occasion Alicia and her husband had been guests at a reception given in their honour by an official of the foreign office. There were perhaps fifty people in all, most of the men in uniform, the women flashily overdressed. The party was well under way when there was a slight current of excited comment, a sudden quietus, and he was there, the much feared, fawned on, and hated Hermann Goering.

He was flanked by two rigidly correct young aides who stayed constantly a pace behind him. He was wearing one of his musical-comedy uniforms, this time in white with much braid, cross sashes, and rows and rows of medals. The glitter, the colour, the belts, sashes, and straps accented the enormous bulk of his flabby figure until he appeared preposterously gross.

He moved through the room, bowing and smiling, a word here, a whisper there. The host was beside him, making introductions, and they came to Alicia and her husband. Even before the formal introduction had been made, Goering had grasped Alicia by the hand. His flesh was soft, full, and unpleasantly moist, and he closed both of his hands over her own slender fingers, half caressing them as he looked steadily at her. He asked again for her name, repeated it carefully to himself, and still gazing steadily into her dark eyes, told her how pleased he was to see her in Berlin, that he hoped she would come often, and perhaps, if it could be arranged, they might dine together.

She was repulsed by his soft face, the quivering cheeks and chins, the wet, full, petulant lips, the pomaded hair. and the strong perfume. But she smiled her thanks, told him that she hoped she might often visit Berlin and that she would be more than honoured to dine with him at some future date.

The Air Marshal lifted one of his hands and reached for Alicia's husband, drew him close, and commented to the effect that he was not only a good businessman but a great judge of feminine beauty. The Air Marshall's other flabby hand, still holding Alicia's, gave it a slight squeeze.

She smiled at him, thanked him for his compliments, and withdrew her hand. He made a quick, stiff bow and moved away.

There had been other parties, large and small dinners, luncheons; and there were always people of prominence and influence. But the talk was guardedly general. Still there were fascinating bits of information available. Oblique references indicated that Allied broadcasts were getting through to the German people; and, though anyone caught listening to such broadcasts might be put to death, there were apparently those who did listen quite regularly.

Alicia made contact with one or two pre-war friends in the international set, but they had been disappointingly unrewarding. They were too fearful of saying anything. They distrusted everyone around them, servants, clerks, even other friends and family, to such an extent there was little to discuss other than past events of the pre-war world. And yet even this bit of negative intelligence was of value to us as indicating how far the rot of Nazi oppression and terror had progressed.

Then came the blow.

Quite suddenly, with no prior warning, Alicia's husband died of a heart attack.

Germany. The bright prospect of expanding activity in Berlin. The infiltration of the Nazi world at its heart. Even the potential development of the contact with the great Hermann Goering. All of this was finished for Alicia with the sudden death of her husband. All this.

But not her career as an agent.

Within three months of her husband's death, Alicia had an apartment in German-occupied Paris with the young German colonel.

General Donovan was intrigued and delighted by Alicia's resourcefulness. In my own mind I never felt quite comfortable with this switch. It introduced a new dimension into Alicia's possible effectiveness as an agent. If she were using the German colonel as a means to an end, if he were only a segment in a coolly calculated plan to continue her clandestine operations from enemy-occupied Paris, well and good. But if there was an element of love, if she was infatuated with the colonel, how sure could we be that she would remain *our* agent, a reliable source?

General Donovan had confidence in her as a personal friend of long standing, and he was certain that her loyalty would withstand even the strain of a love affair. What I apparently had not reckoned with was Alicia's basic character and make-up. She was a natural as an agent. Intrigue, deceit, manipulation, and control, these apparently meant more to her than love. They were life itself, the things for which she lived. The persons involved only made the game exciting; they did not really create an emotional factor.

She was a clever girl. The very fact that she would now be operating from Paris, from enemy-occupied territory, meant that our communication, hers and mine, would undergo some kind of change. After all, she had had no training in shortwave radio transmission or radio code. I could see us frustrated, with an intelligent agent, a daring agent in the middle of Paris, literally bedded down with a Nazi colonel, and yet unable to make use of any of the information she might obtain simply because she could not get it out.

Alicia supplied the answer to that. Our old lines of communication continued, slightly irregular, more widely spaced in time, but they continued. Alicia had managed to convince her German colonel that for a widow of property, with interests in Sweden, frequent trips back to Stockholm would be necessary. Her reports came in as before.

They were vastly rewarding. With plenty of money to spend, not only ours but hers as well, Alicia maintained a miniature salon in Paris where all of the rank of the German hierarchy were welcome. She knew who was in Paris, and why. She knew who was expected, and why. And she knew who was being withdrawn, and why. Cleverly she had fostered a complete disregard of her English connections, until many of the German contacts she made were completely unaware of them. She was accepted as a pro-Axis Swedish widow with money, beauty, wit, and charm beyond the usual. As a result the luncheons and dinners in the elegant apartment off the Avenue Foch were gay, relaxed, and highly informative.

Over the months Alicia got for us vital information establishing troop movements and the reasons behind them. Nazi morale, estimates of air strength, supply hazards, personality conflicts, and dozens of related items that helped us more and more to anticipate the Nazi moves and potentials, these we got through Alicia. Only in one area was there a carefully preserved silence. No one, not even her young colonel himself, could be persuaded to make any statement that could be considered derogatory of Hitler or the Nazi high command. Not that it wasn't there. We know now that it was. But so great was the fear, even among the highest-ranking officers, that criticism of Hitler could mean torture and death that there was not once a mention of him that Alicia could report as unfavourable.

Alicia continued operating as a clandestine agent of the OSS up to the liberation of Paris.

It was then that her young German colonel showed himself for the gentleman and hero he was not. With the Allied troops advancing on Paris, with the fever of the impending liberation of the city building up, he simply vanished. He left Alicia's apartment one morning ostensibly to go to his usual headquarters assignment, and she never saw him again. No word. No message. No contact, direct or indirect, of any kind. Nothing. Whether he was killed in some minor skirmish or major battle; whether he ended his own life in the classic German manner of the "honourable" suicide; or whether he was taken prisoner and lost to view in the general disintegration of the war, we will never know.

Three days after the liberation of Paris I had made contact with Alicia. Off the Avenue Foch, elegantly isolated in a smartly tranquil corner of Paris, her apartment was a serene counterpoint to the war madness, the liberation frenzy, the conflicting emotions of a long-oppressed city at last free.

We sat at tea and talked of the excitement of the past few days. And already there was a singular detachment beginning to show. It was much as if one had only been passingly touched by history, and not been a part of it. It was over for her, and she accepted the fact without emotion. She was neither glad nor sad, uninvolved. Only one thing bothered her: the sudden abandonment of her by the young German colonel. Not that she loved him, there was obviously no hurt there, but her pride had been touched, scarred. It left that chapter of her life unfinished, hanging; and she resented it. Nothing more.

She would have liked to go on. She was ready to do anythink we asked of her; and, yet, she was clever enough to realize that the setting was no longer there for her type of mission, that she had had a special value that demanded equally special circumstances. They no longer existed.

She stayed on in Paris until the autumn, holding to the excitement of the war, letting herself down easily and gradually to the life she would find waiting either in Sweden or England or wherever she decided to settle. I saw her frequently in Paris; she had discovered more and more friends among the Allied forces, until her apartment became a highly select rendezvous. They knew nothing of her career as an agent, her friends. They only assumed that she had been caught up by the war in Paris and had survived it all until the liberation. She chose to let them go on holding this assumption.

I can remember one evening when someone commented to her that it must have been a "bloody bore" to have had to sit out the war in German-occupied Paris.

"I loathed every minute of it," Alicia replied. She was looking directly at me as she spoke; and there was the slightest trace of a wink, an amused sparkle in the dark eyes.

It was several months later that I was able to see Alicia at work as the professional agent.

I was supposed to be flying back to London from Paris, but the drizzle and fog of early November had cancelled all flights, and I found myself re-routed to the Paris-Calais-Dover train and boat trip. It was crowded, the train, and it was a predominantly military group of passengers. But the French had already organized the trains. There was the usual ticket arrangement for meals that assured one a place for a given sitting, and I made my way to the *wagon-restaurant* at the proper time. There was one empty space, at the far end of the car; and I could see two officers and a well-dressed woman already at the table towards which the steward was leading me.

The woman was Alicia.

She quite obviously had seen me even before I had noticed her, and she had raised a protective hauteur to her carriage that informed me of the set-up. I approached with caution.

"I am Mrs Brown." She smiled discreetly and held forth a gloved hand. "And this is Colonel X and Major Y. They are travelling separately, and we have only just been introduced. And you are. . . ?" She paused, waiting for me to fill in the name. "Colonel All. . . . Colonel Alcorn, yes. Do join us. I think it's so much nicer to know one's companions at table. I hate sitting in that stiff, ignoring silence so many people affect."

Alicia had completely taken over the table. And while I sat amused and amazed, Alicia wove a tale for the benefit of the two officers that was completely disarming. She was going home to England for the first time since the beginning of the war, went her tale. She had been caught in France at the outbreak of hostilities, and she had lived quietly and frugally in a remote corner of the country. She really knew little of what had gone on; she had lost all touch with her family and friends in England, and she knew not what she would find when at last she reached home. It was all believable, innocent and just heart-wrenching enough to create sympathy.

Colonel X, an obvious retread from the first World War, a rather pompous, chesty individual with grey hair and a small, clipped moustache on a magenta face, rose to the bait. He would be delighted to be of any assistance possible. He was in a staff position, he assured us all, a liaison job that gave him much scope for making contacts with the British and the French.

Alicia's dark eyes widened with admiration, and he responded with more information as to his importance. She asked about his ribbons as if she had never seen a decoration in her life, and he explained each one with a kind of "aw, shucks" bravado-modesty that was embarrassing. By the end of the lunch we all knew his unit, its location, its position and rate of progress from the landings forward to the present, and many related facts that any basically discreet officer would never have divulged. We were still at war; the horror and the challenge of the Battle of the Bulge was yet to break unexpectedly on us; and yet here was a full colonel of the U.S. Air Force holding forth to a group of chance acquaintances on a train with a lot of information that should have been left undefined.

This sophisticated woman, posing convincingly as a helpless, untravelled, unworldly creature from the English provinces, beguiled one rather pompous American colonel into a kind of momentary slavery. On the boat crossing of the channel he never left her side; and she calmly, flatteringly, and efficiently worked on him. An innocent question about just how some particular thing might have been done, and the colonel took off with descriptions of sorties, encounters with the enemy, and the like. Names dropped like flies. Place names and personalities, these appeared in context until one might have thought the colonel had covered everything from St.-Lô, Coutances. Caen, and Ste.-Mère Église to Paris with everyone from Eisenhower and Montgomery to Rommel and von Runstedt. It was a virtuoso performance, and much of it was obviously braggadocio. But to one seeking information, to a trained agent looking for ever more detail to bolster intelligence gleanings, it was incredibly revealing. From a colonel in the American forces, in the midst of a still desperate war, it was inexcusable.

Alicia filed a full report on the colonel. It was the job of an expert; and as it had only to be carried across London to reach me, it was completely indexed as to what items were gross security violations. A summary of the report was sent on to General Donovan, who in turn made it available to the proper authorities.

Colonel X was quite suddenly airlifted back to the United States. There was disciplinary action and a desk job. I've often wondered if he ever connected his quick return to the States with the attractive dark-eyed woman he had met on a French train.

It was Alicia's last official act for the OSS.

Of all the clandestine agents with whom I was associated during the war, Alicia has crossed my path more often and more unexpectedly than any other.

The first time was some seven years after we had said a formal farewell in London. I had been staying with English friends in British East Africa, and shortly before my departure there was a formal dinner party in Government House in Nairobi. It was the usual minuet, the table seating plan displayed in the entrance hall, each guest formally announced as he entered the drawing-room, much colour, many jewels, and the rest. There were perhaps twenty in all.

There was another couple announced (the names meant nothing), and then suddenly I recognized her. The black hair, the glistening black eyes, the pale, pale skin, the elegance of manner, carriage, and dress, and the jewels. It was Alicia.

Other than a murmured, "Yes, I think we have met," there was nothing about the introduction to indicate we had ever said more than three words to each other.

During the evening I discovered that her new husband, considerably older than she, was a Swiss; and she was again living "in the world", everywhere and anywhere. She was especially anxious to know what had brought me to East Africa, and she found the perfectly honest explanation that I was there on a private visit difficult to credit. The more I protested I had just come on a trip, the more convinced she became that I must be there on some clandestine mission. And as we talked, I found myself becoming equally suspicious of her. I told her so, and we both laughed.

Then, as the evening ended and we were saying good night, she made a last oblique probe. I smiled as I insisted again that I was privately there.

"But there is just one thing I should like to see before I go back to the States," I taunted. "That is your report back to whomever you work for as to just what Alcorn is doing in East Africa."

Her reply was quick and to the point, and it was delivered with blazing black eyes.

"Well, just what the hell *are* you doing here?"

Neither of us will ever believe the other could have been there innocently.

The next time it was Venice.

She was alone. The Swiss had either died or been divorced, I never found out definitely which.

Again I was staying with friends; and there was one of those tremendous, wildly chic, and completely international balls that only Venice can produce. The war was a long way off, and everything to do with it had long since been forgotten. Then, suddenly, in the midst of the glitter, the music, the chatter, the confusion, she was there. We were introduced, and I asked her to dance. It was the first time I had ever danced with her; and, as we whirled around the floor, I found it difficult to believe that this was the same person who had, some fifteen years previously, been a clandestine agent for the OSS. We laughed about it all, and she could hardly remember the name she was using at the time.

It brought her to a discussion of her marriages; and for the first time I discovered that she had, briefly, after the war, been married to an American, but that had been a mistake, except that it had given her an inside look at New York. Then, with her usual wit, perhaps sensing my attempt to go over the changes of name that had occurred in her life, she commented on the difficulties of multiple marriage.

"I've had the full alphabet put on all of my personal things. It's so much easier." She held up a gold compact or *minau-*

dière, and the full alphabet was elegantly inscribed on a small corner panel.

Alicia still held her charm, her wit, her looks.

The last time I saw her was three years ago.

It was in London, and this time it was sad. It was at a large coming-out party, and she was there with a young man some twenty-five years her junior. She had aged (perhaps by contrast with her escort), and her hair was bleached to a honey colour and piled into grotesque pouffe on her head. The sleek, black elegance of her former coiffure, the striking thing about her that made every head turn, was gone, and there was only this beauty-parlour caricature.

But the skin, perhaps a trifle more lifeless and showing an occasional line, was still that incredible pale tissue; and the eyes were snappingly black, the more so for the ridiculous blonde hair. There were more jewels than ever, emeralds and diamonds in a carefully accented arrangement of bracelets, clips, necklace, earrings, and rings. Still elegant.

I danced with her, and then we sat alone at a table for perhaps half an hour before the rather effeminate young man came back to be with her. There was no reference to the war, other than her comment on the death of General Donovan. Theirs had been a friendship of long standing, and she had found nothing to replace it.

Later in the evening, without letting on that I had ever met the woman, I asked someone who the rather handsome blonde with the black eyes might be, the one with the very young escort, and I nodded in the direction of Alicia.

"That's the old Countess X. Napoleonic title. Married to a Frenchman, last I heard, though that may be finished. She's had six or eight husbands. Older than God. Spanish orginally, I believe. Had an English husband somewhere along the line. Awful bore. Gone a bit potty now. Always surrounded by a collection of young men, young enough to be her sons. And talks about what she did in the war. Starts everything with, 'During my war service. . . .' Some service. Must have done most of it on her back."

How little people really know.